Helping Gifted Children Soar:

A Practical Guide
for Parents and Teachers

Carol A. Strip, Ph.D.
with Gretchen Hirsch

Great Potential Press, Inc.
(formerly Gifted Psychology Press, Inc.)
P.O. Box 5057
Scottsdale, AZ 85261
www.giftedbooks.com

Helping Gifted Children Soar: A Practical Guide for Parents and Teachers

Cover Design: ATG Productions, Inc.
Interior Design: Spring Winnette

Published by **Great Potential Press, Inc.**
(formerly Gifted Psychology Press, Inc.)
P.O. Box 5057
Scottsdale, AZ 85261
www.giftedbooks.com

Printed and Bound in the United States of America

05 04 03 02   5 4 3

Library of Congress Cataloging-in-Publication Data

Strip, Carol Ann, 1945-
  Helping gifted children soar: a practical guide for parents and teachers / Carol Strip with Gretchen Hirsch.
    p. cm.
  Includes bibliographical references (p.). and index.
  ISBN 0-910707-41-3
  1. Gifted children--Education (Elementary) 2. Education, Elementary--Parent participation. I. Hirsch, Gretchen. II. Title.

LC3993.22 .S87 2000
371.95--dc21

                                                      00-034756

ISBN 0-910707-41-3

Dedicated
to my talented daughter

Lori Renée Strip

Acknowledgments

Carol Strip would like to acknowledge:

My parents, Harold and Marion Gillespie, who have always modeled the kind of committed parenting and teaching described in this book; my brother and sister-in-law, Gary and Elaine Gillespie, who offered many words of encouragement; my nephew, Brian Gillespie, and my nieces, Julie Gillespie and Angela Newton, for their inspiration and trust; my current and former students, for bringing life, joy, and the love of learning to the classroom; the many graduate teachers I have been privileged to teach; Stanley Fish, who came into my life at the perfect time to inspire the conclusion of this book; Barry Keenan, who has taught me many things about the world of the gifted adult; Alan Jones, who gave me the creative spirit to think "outside the box"; my current principal and friend, Linda Gregg, and our superintendent, Bill Reimer, whose support of gifted children is what makes our program strong; Karen Goebbel, Connie Makely, Dennis Claypool, Sherrie Thompson, Sue Harnden, and Jill Oglesby, my friends and colleagues; Ace Strip, for always being my rock; Steve Brandehoff, my true inspiration and model; Frank Deaner, a real diplomat; Alex Kushkin, who radiates giftedness; Larry Miller, who initiates ideas; Jim Boyd, for his Jack-in-the-box story; Richard Pizzuti, for his steady reassurance; Ryan, Scott, and Kim Pizzuti; Karen and Adrienne Rapp and Bob Maibach, who so generously allowed me to use their stories; my next-generation family, Michael and Julie Taus, who have given me two beautiful granddaughters, Nikki and Shelynn. And, of course, my thanks to you, the readers of this book. It is with much gratitude and love that I offer you this part of my life. Remember that this is a story of hope, and it could be your story.

Gretchen Hirsch would like to acknowledge:

My son, Stew, daughter, Tobey, and grandsons, Tommy and Tyler, for being living examples of giftedness; my daughter-in-law, Lisa, for giving me the gift of time with the boys; Scott Huntley, for sharing his insights and humor; Evie and Doug McCord, for their constant support; Angela Palazzolo, for being the real impetus behind this book; Hank Griffith, Sr., for his contributions on disadvantaged gifted students; Sheila Lewis, for being a superb sounding board; literary agent Jeff Herman, for his efforts in behalf of this book; Jim Webb and his staff at Gifted Psychology Press, Inc., for their patience and insistence that this book be all it should be; and Tony, my gifted husband and friend.

Preface

Near the end of the movie *Forrest Gump*, Forrest discovers he has a young son. In one of the film's most affecting scenes, Forrest, who is slow, asks Jenny, the child's mother, "Is he smart? Or is he like me?"

Certainly Forrest Gump is an unusual father, but in some ways he's Everyparent. When children arrive on the scene, moms and dads are usually excited, sometimes apprehensive, and always curious. Did she inherit Grandma's brown eyes and musical aptitude or Grandpa's nose and manual dexterity—or both? Will he be chatty like his father or introspective like his mother? And all parents want to know what Forrest wanted to know: is my child smart?

If you've picked up this book, you're asking a further question, one I've heard from hundreds of parents over the years. "I know my child is bright," they say, "but is she gifted? I suspect she's more intellectually capable than other children. Am I right?"

I've fielded the same question from scores of teachers who notice that a particular child stands out from the others, maybe in all areas of the curriculum or maybe in only one or two.

One father describes it this way:

> *"His name is Jack and he lives in a box. It appears that he doesn't like the box because he keeps popping out. Whenever he does, everyone seems surprised. Some*

people try to figure out why Jack pops out, while others try to explain why he should stay in, and nearly everyone pushes and shoves until Jack is forced back into the box.

"Once Jack has returned to his box, people begin to play the same old tune; Jack tolerates it as long as he can, but soon, out he pops again. And everyone rushes to stuff him back where he belongs.

"If all these people watched Jack over a period of time, they'd notice that he emerges from his box less and less often. One day, he'll stop popping out altogether."

In the United States, there may be as many as three million children, identified and unidentified, who are just like Jack—children whose intellect outruns our expectations and may exceed their own social and emotional development. And every one of them is a child at risk. In the classroom, teachers are often ill-equipped to deal with these exceptionally bright, emotionally intense children. They find it more comfortable to treat gifted children like everybody else and to ignore their advanced abilities.

At home, the parents of gifted children struggle with the demands of rearing children who at one moment want to discuss the morality of war and at the next are inconsolable because they've broken a favorite pencil or have discovered that the tooth fairy isn't real.

Gifted children are a puzzle, to be sure, but if teachers and parents continually try to stuff them into society's pre-determined boxes, these children—who should be our nation's treasure—may be at risk of becoming society's burdens.

Bored and frustrated by schools that often don't challenge them and by families who often are puzzled by them, gifted children sometimes become anti-social or "behavior problems" who may end up in the medical/psychological establishment or in the justice system.

The key to keeping gifted children on track is for parents and teachers to work together to nurture them—to allow them to "pop out" of their boxes and to exercise and develop their intellectual gifts in an atmosphere that also supports their emotional and social needs.

Both teachers and parents must identify—and equally important, not misidentify—gifted children, because these children have special needs, no less than those affected by physical or learning disabilities. To help gifted children succeed both in school and in life, teaching methods and home strategies must be adapted to take into account these students' unusual intellectual strengths, learning styles, and emotional requirements.

These children have been part of my life for the more than thirty years I've been in the classroom. Teaching gifted children is a true vocation for me, and these wonderful students are the reason I stay in the classroom. To teach is to follow my heart and reap the greatest benefit of my profession. The joy comes from knowing that I have touched the lives of so many gifted children and their parents.

I first wanted to become a teacher when I was four years old. My "school" was attended by a wide assortment of stuffed animals. I named them all, lined them up alphabetically, and pretended to teach them various lessons and skills, starting with Dick and Jane and ending with the study of the stars. My older brother used to sit out of sight and listen to me as I conducted my lessons. He took great pleasure in my antics, laughing especially hard when I disciplined my "students" for talking out of turn.

Later, I found out that life in a real classroom was definitely more complicated than what I had created as a child. For one thing, I soon realized that it was important for me to form a bond not only with my students, but also with their parents if the children were to have the best chance for academic and social success. I've always viewed the parents of my students as partners in education and living because they are as concerned as I about providing the best possible atmosphere for the child, at school and at home.

And that's the reason I've written this book. It's designed to encourage a positive relationship between parents and teachers, because the adults are, after all, teammates in dealing with children's academic, emotional, and social needs.

As both a parent and a teacher of gifted children, I've experienced relationships with these children from both sides. I hope this book will help as you go about the most exciting, exhausting, and exhilarating jobs you'll ever be called upon to do—parenting and teaching a gifted child.

Note: *To protect the privacy of individuals, all children's names and other identifying characteristics have been changed, and some student examples are composites of similar case studies.*

Table of Contents

Section One

An Introduction To Giftedness

Chapter 1

The World's Biggest, Highest, Longest Roller Coaster

Parenting a gifted child is like living in a theme park full of thrill rides. Sometimes you smile. Sometimes you gasp. Sometimes you scream. Sometimes you laugh. Sometimes you gaze in wonder and astonishment. Sometimes you're frozen in your seat. Sometimes you're proud. And sometimes the ride is so nerve-racking, you can't do anything but cry.

Any and all of these reactions are normal, depending on your child and his development. Gifted children are an enormous challenge for parents. These children go through the same developmental stages that other children do, but not in the same way. One part of the child—the cognitive, or thinking, ability—is "older" than the other parts of the personality. This situation is called "asynchronous development" because the child's intellect is out of "sync" with his less developed emotional, social (and sometimes physical) abilities. Asynchronous development can leave a gifted child, as well as parents or teachers, feeling stymied, frustrated, baffled, puzzled, and confused.

Imagine, if you can, that you are five years old, but you can think like a fourth-grader. Where do you find your friends? The five-

year-olds are too immature, and the ten-year-olds don't take you seriously. If they want you around at all, it's as a sort of mascot, not as a
peer. Physically, you can't do the things the fourth-graders can: you
can't hit a ball very well; you have trouble riding a two-wheeler; you
can't run as fast as they can. No matter how hard you try, you'll
always be behind the physical and emotional curve set by your older
classmates. It's like being a person who speaks only German and
travels to Italy and France. You like being there, but because the language and cultures are different, it's hard to be understood and to get
what you need.

Gifted children are part of neither one of their so-called peer
groups, and they are subject to teasing, put-downs, and ridicule
from both children and adults. It's no wonder, then, that they sometimes feel "out-of-whack," weird, inept, and angry. Their emotions,
already exquisitely sensitive, are exposed, raw, and tender, and their
lack of emotional maturity can make their lives—and yours—a
challenge at best and a nightmare at worst.

Gifted children have many wonderful, enjoyable qualities, but
when those qualities are combined with emotional and social imma-
turity, the flip side of those same attributes can look less appealing:

The Ups and Downs of Giftedness

Strength	The Flip Side	Possible Consequences
Comprehension is much greater than that of age-mates.	Finds age-mates' reasoning and comprehension silly—and says so.	Other children avoid the child; adults find him or her "mouthy." The child loses friends.
Language abilities are advanced for her age.	Talks "above" age-mates, who don't understand what the child is talking about. The child talks too much, not allowing others their turns.	Other children perceive the child as snooty and superior and exclude him or her. The child is lonely.
Creative in thinking.	Solves problems his or her own way, rather than the way prescribed by the teacher.	Teacher can feel threatened, view the child as disrespectful of authority, and decide to "clamp down," which sets the stage for rebellion.
Quick in thinking.	Easily bored with routine work and may not complete it. On the other hand, may zip through the work and bounce around the classroom, looking for something else to do.	The teacher may decide the child is inattentive, negative, or a behavior problem who has a bad influence on other children.
High energy level.	May be very distractible, into everything and finishing nothing.	The child can also be worn out by trying to take on too many projects at once. High energy also may be mistaken for attention deficit hyperactivity disorder (ADHD). Medication may be suggested to "calm the child down."
Great powers of concentration.	Sometimes stays too long on one project; gets lost in detail and misses deadlines.	Poor grades, because assigned work is not completed, causing frustration for the child, parents, and teachers.
Adult-level thinking.	Adult-level thinking not accompanied by adult-level social skills, such as tact. May say rude or embarrassing things.	Both children and adults may think the child is rude and avoid him or her altogether.

On the Web site for the National Association for Gifted Children (www.nagc.org), a gifted person is defined as "someone who shows, or has the potential for showing, an exceptional level of performance in one or more areas of expression." These areas may include: *specific academic abilities, general intellectual ability, creativity, leadership, and the visual and performing arts.*

Joseph Renzulli, a pioneer in the field of gifted education, describes gifted characteristics this way:

> *"Gifted behavior reflects an interaction among three basic clusters of human traits—these clusters being above average general or specific abilities, high levels of task commitment, and high levels of creativity.... Persons who manifest, or are capable of developing, an interaction among the three clusters require a wide variety of educational opportunities and services that are not ordinarily provided through regular instructional programs."[1]*

Other experts in the field have gone beyond Renzulli's three clusters to develop a variety of published lists that define common characteristics of gifted children. Checklist items from these lists are frequently used as a screening tool to determine whether a child should be tested for inclusion in gifted programs. Barbara Clark, author of *Growing Up Gifted: Developing the Potential of Children at Home and at School*, and many other educators include at least the following traits:

- overwhelming curiosity
- flexible thought processes
- ability to form and ask probing questions
- exceptional memory
- independence in thought and action
- knowledge about many different subjects
- logical thinking processes
- originality
- extreme sensitivity to the expectations and feelings of others

[1]Sternberg, R. J. & Davidson, J. (Eds.). (1986). *Conceptions of giftedness.* New York: Cambridge University Press.

- intensity
- idealism
- creativity in areas of interest
- keen sense of humor
- feeling of being different
- highly developed sense of justice and moral judgment
- ability to identify inconsistencies between ideas and behavior
- perfectionism[2]

Linda Silverman, director of the Gifted Development Center in Denver, Colorado, an organization that provides programs and support for highly gifted children and their families, adds that gifted children:

- have long attention spans (if they're interested in something)
- exhibit exceptional energy
- read early, or enjoy being read to, if they are unable to read
- question authority
- show great imagination
- demonstrate skill at jigsaw puzzles

One or two traits may not constitute giftedness, but a whole collection of these characteristics suggests that the child is gifted.

Many gifted children are highly creative, but creativity is hard to define and harder still to measure. Some experts feel that creativity must involve a product, that is, something that has been created—a song, poem, dance, performance, theory, or work of art. E. Paul Torrance, designer of the *Torrance Tests of Creative Thinking*, states:

[2]Clark, B. (1988). *Growing up gifted: Developing the potential of children at home and at school (Fifth Edition)*. Upper Saddle River, NJ: Merrill.

"Some degree of creativity occurs whenever a person solves a problem for which he/she had no previously learned or practiced solution. Some solutions ... require only tiny creative leaps, while others call for genuine breakthroughs in thinking. All of them require that individuals go beyond where they have ever gone before."[3]

Jane Piirto, director of the talent development program at Ashland University in Ashland, Ohio, adds, "The creative personality can be either developed or thwarted. ... Everyone is creative. Those who are more creative have learned to be so."[4] Whatever creativity is, most experts believe that parents, teachers, and communities must provide opportunities for students to exercise their instincts to think new thoughts and make new things.

Giftedness can manifest itself through the visual and performing arts. Obviously, those who are talented in these areas will demonstrate exceptional ability in areas such as music, dance, art, acting, scenic design, costuming, and other skills related to these fields.

Leadership likewise can be an aspect of giftedness. Leadership traits involve outstanding abilities in areas such as written or oral communication, decision-making, problem solving, working in groups, and planning.[5]

Just as there are many hues in the spectrum, there are also many gradations of giftedness. Most gifted children are highly able in one or two areas, such as math, science, or music, but may be less capable in other subjects. However, there are a few who appear to be gifted across the board, exceptional at everything they do.

Gifted children are found in every ethnic and socio-economic group. The gifted may also include children with a wide variety of disabilities—including many types of physical disabilities, such as cerebral palsy; vision, speech or hearing impairments; or specific learning disabilities; and sometimes it's hard to get school officials to look beyond the "handicapping condition" to also recognize the giftedness. Gifted children are already exceptional children; gifted

[3]Torrance, E. P. & Goff, K. (1989). A quiet revolution. *Journal of Creative Behavior*, pp. 2, 23, 136-145.
[4]Piirto, J. (1998). *Understanding those who create* (Second Edition). Scottsdale, AZ: Gifted Psychology Press.
[5]Karnes, F. A. & Chauvin, J. C. (2000). *Leadership development program manual*. Scottsdale, AZ: Gifted Psychology Press.

children with a handicapping condition are sometimes called "twice exceptional." These students deserve to receive services in both areas of exceptionality.

Highly gifted children, those with exceptionally high IQs (145 to 160+), constitute a special subset within the group of gifted children and are the prodigies the media are quick to recognize. To explain briefly, if children are "moderately" gifted, they will surely benefit from learning at a faster pace and with greater depth of instruction, special resource rooms, grouping with other bright students, and various other program or curricular options, and generally they can navigate the school environment successfully most of the time. A highly gifted child, on the other hand, may be out of place in the day-to-day schoolhouse. He may need an individually tailored curriculum, university courses, mentors, tutors, or even a special school. In fact, highly gifted children are as different from "moderately" gifted children as "moderately" gifted children are from average students.

A Quick Look at Some Gifted Children

Your child's unusual abilities, although a blessing in many ways, also set the stage for all sorts of misunderstandings at home and at school, and the misunderstood child is frequently upset. As the child's parents, you get to see the worst behavior she has to offer. You may experience the child's tears, tantrums, and irrational fears. Kermit the Frog used to say, "It's not easy being green." Well, it's not easy being gifted, either, and it's definitely a challenge to be the parent or the teacher of a gifted child.

There is a common belief that gifted children are compliant, peaceful, studious, industrious, interested in a wide variety of hobbies, and able to fit in well at school. And sometimes that's true. Many gifted children are winsome and delightful to be around. But sometimes these children are puzzling, challenging, and frustrating. The following examples help describe the diversity within gifted children.

Arlene

Arlene, a third-grader, was so admired by her age-mates that when she absentmindedly wore two different-colored socks to school one day, almost every other little girl in the class followed suit within a week. Arlene had unknowingly initiated a fad.

Along with her intellectual attributes, Arlene had another special quality common to gifted children, a quality nurtured extensively by her mother. That quality was empathy. Arlene had great sensitivity to the needs and insecurities of other children; she went out of her way to include those who might otherwise have been left behind. She was very popular and, at the same time, quite modest about her own talents. The other children admired her and considered her a leader.

Grace and Willie

Tenth-graders Grace and Willie were twins, both gifted, but in different areas. Grace was talented in art and mathematics, Willie in literature and language. Their parents, who immigrated to the United States just before the children were born, had always emphasized the importance of family and responsibility. They worked hard to make sure the children appreciated each other's talents and insisted that Grace and Willie learn to cooperate, rather than compete. Grace tutored Willie in math; Willie led his sister through the intricacies of poetry. They both took piano lessons and helped each other master difficult passages of music. Because they had learned to be kind and cooperative at home, they brought the same traits into the classroom, where they were popular with teachers and students alike. They currently attend different universities, but are still close friends and continue to be well liked by nearly everyone they meet.

Kevin

Nine-year-old Kevin was a math whiz. Since mathematics is a rather sequential activity, it's an ideal subject for independent programmed learning, and Kevin's resource teacher made sure he had every opportunity to move ahead as quickly as he wished. Her belief in his abilities gave him a great deal of confidence, which helped him in his social life. He became sure of himself without being arrogant and was always very willing to help other students who were having difficulty in math.

In the sixth grade, Kevin expressed a desire to take the SAT, so his teacher arranged for him to tackle a series of practice tests prior to the actual examination. He did extremely well even though he was a full year younger than other students when he took the test; in fact, he received a perfect score on the math section. Surprising to him, but not to his teacher, was the fact that he also received a perfect score on the verbal portion of the test. Although he was understandably proud of his accomplishment, he wasn't boastful, and he accepted the congratulations of his classmates with modesty.

· · · · ·

The gifted children described above have been able to strike a balance between high achievement and equally advanced social competence. These children were able to operate successfully within the school system without a great deal of intervention. Yet for every child like Grace or Kevin or Arlene, there is another very bright child whose behavior is disconcerting, confusing, or even heart-breaking. Gifted students' academic abilities are not always combined with well-developed social and emotional skills, as the next examples illustrate.

Jenny

Six-year-old Jenny was one of the most highly gifted children her teacher had ever met. Although only a first-grader, Jenny already possessed amazing cognitive powers—she understood many big words and often spoke like an adult. She desperately wanted to express her thoughts in writing, but her fine motor skills were not sufficiently developed for her to handle pencil and paper. Her frustration was enormous and increased her stress, which then led to even greater difficulty in manipulating the tools of writing. The process was so laborious for her that her posture became strained, her hands stiff and claw-like. Her little body shook. It sometimes looked as if she would literally turn herself inside out trying to bend the pencil to her will.

When she was imperfect at writing, Jenny would sob. She was different from the other children to begin with, and her crying made her the butt of jokes and teasing by the other first-graders. "Look at Jenny; she's a baby," was their nearly constant refrain. Jenny's life was tough. Her asynchronous development—that is, the discrepancies among her intellectual, emotional, and physical skills—were the most extreme the teacher had ever encountered.

Jenny's mother was both worried and frightened by the intensity of her daughter's frustrations and emotional outbursts, and she became concerned about Jenny's mental health. Something needed to be done. So Jenny, her teacher, and her mother worked out a strategy that was a secret among the three of them. The teacher provided Jenny with a simple wire device that attached to her pencil and gently held her hand perpendicular to the paper in the proper position for writing, thus preventing her from making a fist and squeezing her pencil too tightly to write. Jenny practiced with this device at home. She also learned to type her words on a computer keyboard, which gave her a relatively rapid way to get her thoughts on paper, easing her frustration at not being able to write.

Put in charge of an important part of her own learning, Jenny worked hard and soon developed the muscle control she needed to use her pen or pencil. When she could manipulate these writing tools successfully, her emotional outbursts decreased in frequency. She was still an unusual child with unusual academic needs, but her emotions were now more manageable, which gave her more time for learning and play.

Jenny's story clearly shows what kind of impact asynchronous development can have on a young child's intellectual and social life. In the fourth grade now, Jenny's social skills have begun to catch up to her scholastic abilities.

Franklin

Franklin was a gifted eighth-grader who, one day, yelled and swore at his teacher. It wasn't a deliberate, calculated thing. He was simply incredibly frustrated by the behavior of his classmates, which he found immature and childish; by the lack of depth in classroom discussion; and by what he considered meaningless, trivial homework assignments. As he walked from one class to another, a teacher who had assigned a paper Franklin thought was a waste of time said, "Hey, Frank, when are you going to turn in that history assignment?"

At this point, Franklin, who hated being called Frank, lost it. He threw his books and papers into the air and verbally assaulted the teacher. His extremely inappropriate and abusive language drew quite a crowd.

Of course, this blow-up wasn't tolerated, and there were consequences that Franklin needed to face. The teachers and administrators looked at Franklin's record and at the type of support that could be expected from his family. Everything was positive. Franklin had never been a discipline problem. His grades were excellent. He participated in extra-curricular activities. His parents were likely to support an intervention that would help Franklin avoid this type of behavior in the future. School personnel didn't feel that this incident was the beginning of a trend toward more acting out, but naturally, they were concerned.

Franklin was an exceptional student, just as students with severe learning or behavior problems are exceptional when compared to average students. His gifted resource teacher advocated for him in the same way that a special education teacher would advocate for children with other types of special needs. The gifted education resource teacher spoke with the classroom teacher and convinced him to drop the suspension he felt Franklin deserved; then, Franklin's parents and school officials worked out a plan that provided appropriate discipline and consequences. The parents enlisted the aid of a mentor whom Franklin respected, and this team worked together to keep Franklin on track.

Franklin's outburst, serious as it was, was not part of a pattern of antisocial behavior, but the result of a day of frustration, non-fulfillment, confusion, and inability to control what was going on in his life. When adults have days like that, they usually refrain from swearing at the boss or throwing all the dishes at the kitchen wall, but Franklin had just turned twelve and hadn't yet learned a full set of coping behaviors to handle stress and frustration. His social and emotional skills, particularly his judgment, lagged behind his intellect.

Now a high school junior, Franklin is taking two courses at a local university. There have been no further eruptions of this type, but his original outburst is typical of gifted children who have a low tolerance for frustration.

Rosa

Like many gifted children, eight-year-old Rosa was curious. She was especially fascinated by forensics and wandered around the neighborhood looking for animal remains, particularly skulls, which she would drag home to study. Her parents thought this fascination with dead things was macabre and were very worried that Rosa might be starting down the path toward animal abuse, witchcraft, or worse. Her teacher was able to help them understand that Rosa wasn't interested in hurting the animals. She wasn't torturing them or setting them on fire. She was busy analyzing the skulls and trying to figure out what had happened to the squirrels and skunks.

Today, Rosa is a doctor specializing in research. She began this career path in childhood, and she was not unusual in this regard. Many gifted children find areas of special interest when they are very young.

Jamaal

Jamaal was a sixth-grade bully, constantly berating other children about their lack of ability as compared to his. "Oh, I read that when I was in first grade," he'd say, or "I already know how to do that." He barged around the room, pushing other children out of his way. He appeared to be an out-of-control child.

Jamaal was a hard case until, bit by bit, his parents and teacher began to discern some "hot buttons" that set him off, and they discovered some areas in which they could channel and refocus his energy. It wasn't that Jamaal wanted to charge around the classroom disrupting everything. He was simply a mass of untapped energy, and because he was unchallenged by material he'd mastered long before, he was using his energy negatively. Understandably, his teacher wasn't happy with his behavior, and deep down, neither was Jamaal.

His teacher discovered that Jamaal liked everything connected with money and economics, so when the gifted resource class did a simulation in which they developed their own business, the teacher made sure Jamaal was given the job of company treasurer. His dad, who happened to be the chief financial officer of a mid-sized corporation, developed some cash flow projection scenarios for Jamaal to use during the project, tying them to the types of plans he had to use in his own job. The charts, graphs, and projections made sense to this young executive-in-training, and he became considerably more agreeable in class.

Jamaal is now in high school. He takes some Advanced Placement courses that challenge him, and he has stopped bragging about his superior intellect. His earlier swaggering was his attempt, although somewhat misguided, to get the academic attention he needed, and like the other students described here, his judgment about what is appropriate behavior was not in tune with what others expected.

Sheila

Sixteen-year-old Sheila was a frequent door-slammer at home. According to Sheila, everything her parents did was wrong, and everything they said was stupid. "Hate" was her favorite word, as in "I hate this house, and I hate you, too!"

Sheila valued her privacy above all things. Her room was her sanctuary. One day, after a loud disagreement with her parents, she stomped into her room and slammed the door. Acting on a plan they'd worked out in advance, her father and mother quickly tapped out the retaining pins that held the door on its hinges.

As Sheila stared, aghast, her father picked up the door and toted it down the hall. "Sheila," he said, his voice controlled and even, "until you can learn to enter your room without slamming the door and upsetting the entire household, you've given up your right to have a door. Once you've learned to treat the rest of the family with the respect we deserve, you may earn back the door and the privacy you deserve."

At the time, Sheila was furious, but she earned her door back. Now grown, she also earned two college degrees in five years and is currently employed as a chemical engineer.

Sheila's teenage rejection of her parents was an outgrowth of a common trait of gifted children—judgmentalism. She tended to hold others to nearly impossible standards and to rebuke them if they didn't measure up. Gifted children can be harsh judges of teachers, friends, society, and especially their parents. It is good to remember that teenagers are also navigating the difficult but necessary transition of separating from parents and becoming young adults. If a gifted child like Sheila is both separating from her parents and is also highly critical of what she sees as their "faults," relationships between the child and parents can become strained and sometimes quite unpleasant.

What these examples teach is that giftedness isn't always pretty. Sometimes it's confusing and downright messy. Of course, gifted children often are inspiring and delightful in their behaviors. But a gifted child can sometimes appear to be an incorrigible, overly emotional, or troubled child. At various ages and stages of development, the same gifted child can be clingy, weepy, dependent, and withdrawn, or rebellious, combative, and defiant.

"Twice-Exceptional" Gifted Children

Some parents and teachers don't realize that children who have disabilities may also be gifted, and are thus "twice-exceptional." For example, a student with vision problems may learn very rapidly and demonstrate a superb memory and well-developed verbal skills; a hearing-impaired child may exhibit a quick mastery of speech-reading and be able to reason quite effectively. Students with other types of physical or emotional disabilities may also have advanced thinking skills and problem-solving abilities, as well as a great deal of creativity.

Children with a specific learning disability such as dyslexia may at the same time have a wonderful vocabulary, keen imagination, and advanced understanding.[6] Often, however, such children view themselves as less able than they really are because they focus on their disability rather than on their strengths.

If parents suspect that their disabled or handicapped child could be gifted or that their gifted child could have a learning disability, it's important that they speak with a psychologist to request testing for more information. A disability may mask a child's giftedness, and conversely, giftedness may hide a child's disability.

A special education resource teacher who works with hearing impaired children in an under-funded rural school system described a second-grade boy who was a student in one of the regular classrooms. The child was easily completing work far above second-grade level in math, yet barely holding his own in reading. His classroom teacher felt this was good enough because, although he was struggling, he was reading only slightly below grade level.

The resource teacher, however, felt that there was more to the story of his variable performance, and so she suggested the child be tested for a possible reading problem. The testing confirmed her suspicions. The boy was suffering from a learning disability related to processing the written word. Once diagnosed, he was given additional help and now is exceptional not only in math but also in reading.

---

[6]Willard-Holt, C. (1999). *Dual exceptionalities*. ERIC EC Digest (E574). Reston, VA: The Council for Exceptional Children.

"I think all teachers want children to succeed, so when you find a student who has it in him to excel, you really want to help," this teacher says. "Sometimes you have to look a little harder to find out what the child really needs. I just had a feeling about this one; he was so unusual."

This story highlights an important clue: If a teacher or parent notices a wide difference between the child's performance in school subjects—for example, between her achievements in math versus reading—it may be a clue that the child has a learning disability in the area that is low. Further testing may be warranted. A learning disability is not the only reason for such discrepancies, however. Gifted children may also underachieve in a particular class simply because they don't like the teacher, are in a power struggle with their parents over schoolwork, or because of other emotional problems.

It's important for teachers and parents to realize that an obvious disability may coexist with that potential for "exceptional level of performance" that is the hallmark of giftedness. This in no way diminishes the giftedness, but means that the child will need to learn ways to compensate for the disability. If this disability is in written language, for example, the child may compensate by taking a tape-recorder to class to help her remember important points and by doing all her writing on a computer. Parents and teachers must also be aware that gifted children may have subtle learning disabilities despite their overall high ability. These may or may not affect the child's overall achievement, though such disabilities tend to cause more problems as the child enters high school years when classroom material becomes more difficult.

Watching for Giftedness

Marcy

Twelve-month-old Marcy was a quiet baby who had never uttered a recognizable word. One day, her mother loaded Marcy into the car to take the child with her on her errands. Mom started the car and drove off down the highway. While mother and daughter waited at a stoplight, a small, soft voice said, "Turn the radio on." Marcy's startled mother turned to see who was speaking; she almost believed someone had climbed into the back seat while the car was stopped at the light. However, Marcy was the only occupant of the back seat, and she smiled when her mom turned on the radio.

Although Marcy's example is unusual because of her very young age, verbal ability is perhaps one of the most common characteristics of giftedness. Many parents of gifted children report that their children spoke earlier or used words and concepts that were more advanced than those of their same-age peers.

Mai Li

Mai Li was three years old when she traveled with her mother to visit her grandparents. At the airport, Mai Li seemed entranced by a wall tapestry that included a complex series of lines and circles. Standing in front of the tapestry, she traced the design with her finger. Later, hurtling across the country in the airplane, she asked for her crayons. As Mai Li drew, her mother realized she wasn't making the random squiggles one would expect of a three-year-old. Instead, she used the entire page to painstakingly reproduce the tapestry pattern that had so intrigued her in the airport lobby. Although still in preschool, Mai Li demonstrated the striking memory, recall, and concentration typical of a gifted child.

Quincy

Quincy was in the second grade. His teacher and his school psychologist both believed that he had Attention Deficit Disorder because his mind often wandered. They recommended to his parents that Quincy see a physician who might evaluate whether medication could increase his ability to stay on-task in the classroom. The teacher told his mother she hoped to get Quincy "where he belonged," and "like the other children" by the end of the school year.

Quincy's class was memorizing facts about the calendar—facts he had known since kindergarten. One day, as he discussed this situation with his mother, Quincy said, "Mom, do you know what I found out? You can take any day on the calendar, add together the days on either side of it, divide that number by two, and the remaining number is the same as the day you chose first."

Wow! No wonder Quincy's teacher thought he couldn't pay attention! Mentally, he had left the rest of the class in the dust. He was unchallenged, bored, and fidgety. However, once he was tested and placed in a program for gifted students, the need for medication was never mentioned again.

Quincy's fascination with mathematics continued; when he took a class in Ancient History in middle school, he researched all he could about Egyptian and Greek numbering systems and then learned to write the numbers in those languages. He worked with an abacus to discern the logic behind the ancient mathematical systems. Soon he was making up his own logic problems to try out on his classmates.

A gifted child's interests are usually sustained over an extended period of time. Quincy's continued involvement with mathematics exemplifies that pattern.

Jake

Jake was eight years old and in the third grade when he was referred to the gifted program. He arrived for testing early, his face expressing fierce determination. He was focused and intense throughout the entire testing period. Finished long before the other students, he brought his test and answer sheet to the teacher's desk.

He said, "I know this test was supposed to measure how we think through a problem, but I went ahead and figured out the exact answers, too. There was no place to put them on this sheet, so I wrote them in the margins." Even though Jake wasn't required to do the math itself, he missed only two questions on a test that was scaled to go up to the sixth-grade level.

In the world of gifted students, high energy, eagerness, and enthusiasm like Jake's are everyday occurrences. In fact, their eagerness to learn is what makes these students such a joy to teach.

* * * * * *

The case histories above are not out of the ordinary. Teachers of gifted children have heard many tales of remarkably advanced ability—usually combined with asynchronous development. Parents relate stories about children who walked confidently at the age of seven months, children who could read at the age of two or three, and children who could add and subtract in ones, tens, and hundreds by the age of five or six.

However, the case histories also show how different these exceptional children can be from one another. It's hard to generalize about gifted students, but there are a few points that are important to understand.

First, gifted children **are children**. Because of the children's mental gifts, parents, teachers and other adults may be tempted to view them as miniature grown-ups. Exceptionally mature in their outlook, gifted children sometimes seem to be old souls. But they aren't. They haven't been on this planet very long. They have little life experience, and they are no more ready to be responsible for themselves than any other child of a similar age. Yes, they can often out-think and out-talk their parents, siblings, teachers, and friends, but their emotional development often lags behind their intellect. And they still need the guidance, discipline, rules of conduct, limits, and boundaries that all children need to feel safe and cared for.

Second, **academically gifted children are out-of-the-box, unusual thinkers**. Their cognitive capabilities far exceed the norms. They have the ability to think and reason analytically at least two, four, or sometimes even more years beyond what would be expected of children the same age. Therefore, it's critical that they be provided with materials, curricula, experience, and discussions that match their interests and abilities—both at home and at school.

It's also crucial that they be allowed to think in their own unique ways, rather than be forced to do every task in an order or sequence expected of another child. Gifted children are uniquely different, and their differences need to be provided for in the classroom and at home.

Chapter 2

Is My Child Gifted—Or Just Smart?

Are Children Smarter Than They Used To Be?

Today's moms and dads have access to much more information about infant and child development than did parents a generation ago. Consequently, there are many children who are products of exceptional parenting. These children have been intellectually stimulated from birth. They've been talked to, read to, and played with. Fortunate children like these have been provided with books, games, puzzles, computer learning, music, and art materials. They've watched *Sesame Street* and other children's programming. By the time they enter kindergarten, they can differentiate shapes and colors and understand concepts such as alike and opposite; they know their letters and numbers. They've visited the zoo, the science center, the movies, and the grocery store. They've eaten in restaurants, perhaps both fast food and "white tablecloth" establishments. They may have been taken to dance and musical performances. Perhaps they've attended both amateur and professional sports events. They might have been active participants in church suppers or neighborhood picnics and festivals. All of these activities give these children things to talk about and learn from.

Some of these little ones have attended *Head Start* or other preschool or day care programs that focus on both learning and self-esteem. Their preschool experience may have included children with various disabilities, so they readily accept those who use sign language or wheel chairs. Many pre-schoolers have also been exposed to an extended family, whether these people are real kinfolk or their parents' friends. Exposure to other people and groups has enriched these children's lives and prepared them for school.

Their health has been guarded, too. They've seen the pediatrician or clinic health care provider regularly, and since most school districts require immunization, the majority of students are up-to-date on their shots. They eat healthful foods, get lots of exercise, and have regular bedtimes. All of these help learning.

Although enrichment opportunities are more readily available to middle-class children, lack of money doesn't have to mean lack of opportunity. It may be difficult, but it is certainly possible for lower income families to find these same advantages, and many do. One minority principal with experience in both inner city and suburban schools says it this way:

> *"Sometimes you have to ask for what you need. Let's be honest. Money makes things easier, but there are ways for parents to get what they need for their children.*
>
> *"The public library is free, and parents can find all sorts of books, tapes, computers, and programs for children. So if parents don't have a computer at home, and they know that the enrichment their child needs involves technology, a library computer can be a substitute. And a librarian can be a wonderful resource to parents. Librarians can help them find books on giftedness so they can be more understanding of their children's special needs, and librarians can also help children discover subjects, authors, and resources that can stretch their minds.*
>
> *"Getting this enrichment for children can be hard. Many inner-city people are working two or three jobs just to survive; the adults need enrichment themselves, and that's where teachers can really help. If they see a*

child who has the potential to excel, teachers can direct both students and parents to community resources they know about. And teachers themselves can talk to community cultural leaders and often get free admission to concerts, theater, or dance performances for children who need enrichment but can't afford a ticket."

Will Enrichment Make a Child Gifted?

Children whose life experience has been enriched in many of these ways come to school ready to learn, and they usually excel in the early grades. They are bright, eager, and often socially adept—the public's (and sometimes parents' and teachers') idea of gifted students. But if the adults watch these children for a period of time, they may notice that by the third or fourth grade, some of the children are "leveling out,"—that is, they're performing like most of their chronological peers. They're still very intelligent, but their intellectual ability is now being challenged by more complex material. Although they may have appeared gifted in kindergarten and first grade, it's now evident that they are simply smart children who have had an enriched early childhood and who will excel in the so-called regular classroom.

Gifted children have a different situation. These children may also have had careful, loving parenting, although they may or may not have received the exceptional opportunities available to families with more resources. But so long as gifted children receive reasonable opportunities to explore, think, and create, their intellectual gifts generally can thrive, sometimes even with relatively little stimulation. Their giftedness is part of the genetic endowment—the potential they brought along with them when they were born. Of course, this needs to be nurtured and encouraged by their parents and others, but it exists by itself.

Introducing children to a wide variety of learning opportunities actually helps identify those who are gifted. For example, suppose a group of young children goes to the museum to look at dinosaur bones. All of the children will be fascinated by the skeletons, but the gifted child may suddenly blurt out that brontosauruses must have been leaf eaters because they had long necks, just like today's giraffes. The gifted child is able to see relationships and make connections that aren't immediately apparent to other children. Gifted children soak up information rapidly and are usually on a constant, intense quest to learn more—and that intensity might be one of the earliest indicators of giftedness.

In spite of what we do or sometimes don't do, gifted children learn in the same way they breathe—automatically. We do not so much teach these children as we expose them to many points of view, a challenging curriculum, role models, and all sorts of possibilities. Gifted children are often autonomous learners and much of what they learn will be self-taught. Still, they need parents and teachers to guide them, particularly because their intellectual development often outpaces their judgment.

Even with all their gifts, these unusually bright children may arrive in the classroom ready to argue and challenge, rather than to learn. Although they may socialize well, more often than not they're somewhat out of step socially with their age-mates. They may try to organize the other children into complex games with elaborate rules. They may question and speak out, defend their own point of view, and correct others. The teacher may consider such traits disrespectful and disruptive and might conclude that these children are spoiled and impertinent rather than gifted.

Just as a smart child who is a hard worker and a high achiever may be mistakenly identified as gifted, a truly gifted child may be labeled as a troublemaker, a nuisance, a classroom pest, or even suspected of having Attention Deficit Hyperactivity Disorder (ADHD). The bright child may end up in the gifted class, the gifted child in the principal's office, and neither of them is in the right place.

Of course, not every sassy, aggressive, acting-out child is gifted; many gifted children are patient, polite, kind, and helpful. Parents and teachers must observe the child over time to know precisely what they're dealing with.

Smart children may indeed be more sophisticated thinkers than children of prior generations simply because they've had more experiences and been exposed to more information earlier in life. Nonetheless, smart children can be overwhelmed by the rigor and demands of a gifted curriculum. Gifted children, on the other hand, generally thrive in this type of creative and challenging environment. In fact, if they don't receive the stimulation they need for their intellectual and social growth, some gifted students will simply "camouflage" and hide their abilities or let their talents wither and die.

Many Children, Many Gifts

Their high potential in many areas is what gifted students have in common. But there are various kinds of giftedness, and gifted children may differ more from each other than they do from their less gifted classmates. Some have strengths in science and math, while some are brilliant poets. Some are disorganized, random thinkers who take on multiple projects, all of which are incomplete; others are organized and systematic, dealing with one task at a time until they've finished them all. Some are very extroverted; others are introverted loners who need time to sit and think. Some have so much energy that they can barely sit still. Others have such intense powers of concentration that they have to be pried away from a seated task. Some are self-motivated, perfectionistic achievers; others, perhaps frightened by what they believe is expected of them, achieve at levels far below their competencies. Some are seriously concerned with rules and issues of right and wrong, while others are class clowns who use their mental equipment to keep things stirred up and lively.

Their learning styles vary as well. *Visual learners* learn best by reading, watching tapes, or studying posters. *Auditory learners* absorb information by listening. These children are comfortable with lectures, discussion, and question and answer sessions.

Kinesthetic learners do best when they are allowed to manipulate ideas and concepts with their hands.

Meeting the learning styles of different children in a classroom is a challenge, but good teachers do it every day. Suppose a third-grade class is studying the solar system. The teacher may show a video and then have a class discussion about space, thus accommodating auditory and visual learners. The children then break into small groups and build scale models of the planets, using facts they've discovered about the planets' size, topography, atmosphere, and unique characteristics. Although all the children will learn from this hands-on scale model activity, the kinesthetic learners will gain the greatest benefits.

Smart or Gifted? Ways To Tell

Smart children. Gifted children. Smart children who look like gifted children. Gifted children who have learning disabilities or are hiding their intellectual powers. The whole issue can be a puzzle, but there are some traits to watch for if you're trying to decide whether a particular child is gifted or simply smart and benefiting from an enriched background. Keep in mind as you read the lists of traits that not every gifted child will exhibit every single trait.

Learning Speed and Application of Concepts	
Smart Children:	**Gifted Children:**
learn in a convergent, linear fashion, piling fact upon fact until they grasp a concept.	think divergently and/or rapidly. In a ten-step process, they may jump directly from Step 2 to Step 10, because by the time they've completed the second step, they've already figured out the problem.

Learning Speed and Application of Concepts

Smart Children:	Gifted Children:
benefit from practice and repetition and are patient with some types of rote learning.	process information in unique ways. They may use "reverse engineering" to solve problems—that is, they gain the answer through intuition and then work back through the steps required to arrive at the initial question.
follow directions well.	dislike drills and rote learning, because they've mastered what they're supposed to learn by the first or second repetition.
take in and understand the information presented in class.	prefer finding new ways to solve problems, but are able to follow directions if necessary. synthesize information presented in class and can apply it to new situations.

Questioning Style

Smart Children:	Gifted Children:
ask questions that have answers.	ask questions about abstract ideas, concepts, and theories that may not have easy answers.
try to gather facts that relate to the current task.	enjoy figuring out relationships, seeing cause and effect, and predicting new possibilities.
may prefer that facts be presented in a sequence they can follow.	like complexity and are sometimes comfortable with ambiguous answers to questions.
may ask the same question more than once.	may ask the same question more than once, but rarely in the same way.

Emotional Outlook	
Smart Children:	**Gifted Children:**
show emotion, but generally are able to get past an upsetting incident fairly easily. They are usually able to articulate what's bothering them and will talk relatively freely about their emotions.	experience heightened, sometimes all-consuming, emotions that may hamper other areas of thought or work. They are passionate and they feel deeply. Some are amazingly empathetic, but may bottle up and internalize their feelings or be afraid to show their emotions.
understand that relationships have ups and downs. They can argue heatedly with a friend, yet be best buddies again by the end of the day.	invest heavily in relationships and can be excessively distraught if those relationships are disturbed by a disagreement, a perceived wrong, or a friend's defection or disloyalty.

When asked how they're feeling, gifted children who are suppressing their emotions usually say they're "fine," even when their outward behavior shows clearly that they aren't fine. If they choose to do so, they can disguise their emotions better than most other children.

Gifted children often push their feelings down because they're frightened to show others what's going on in their inner lives. Their feelings are often so intense that the children wonder if they're "normal." They can feel as if they're holding the ocean in a bottle; they may be afraid that if they take out the stopper, they'll be overwhelmed by the waves—that once they begin to vent their emotions, they won't be able to stop. They fear losing control, and if there's one thing gifted children need, it's a sense of self-control and belonging. So they act as normal and ordinary as possible and tell their parents what they think the parents want to hear. Most of the time, they know precisely what adults want them to say.

Friendships can be problematic. A gifted child may, after long consideration, confide deeply in one friend; that's why the break-up of a friendship can be so devastating. If the friendship falls apart, the child has no outlet for all the emotion previously shared with the lost friend. The child may then grieve deeply or show anger that seems excessive to parents.

Level of Interest

Smart Children:	Gifted Children:
ask questions and are curious about a number of things.	show intense curiosity about nearly everything or often immerse themselves in an area that interests them.
finish projects as assigned.	get deeply involved and may not finish projects on time because they've become engrossed in or distracted by a particular aspect of the assignment. They can become so interested in a specific topic that they ignore other areas.
work hard and energetically.	show so much energy and enthusiasm for their areas of interest that they may dream up their own assignments and projects.
work to please others.	require minimal direction and suggestions.

Language Ability

Smart Children:	Gifted Children:
learn new vocabulary easily, but choose words that are typical for their ages.	use extensive, advanced vocabularies, understand verbal nuances that escape others, enjoy wordplay and puns, and often talk over the heads of their playmates (and sometimes over adults, too).
take turns in conversation because their minds are attuned to the give and take of relationships with others.	can dominate conversations at home or at school because of their intense excitement about ideas, although there are many quietly gifted children who have to be encouraged to share their thoughts.
understand structure of language, and can learn new languages with practice.	learn language skills rapidly. Gifted immigrant students typically learn their new language much faster than other students, sometimes in as little as two months.

Concern with Fairness	
Smart Children:	**Gifted Children:**
state firm opinions about what's fair, but those opinions usually relate to personal situations, such as, "He has more cereal in his bowl than I do."	show concern about fairness and equity far more intensely and on a more global scale. They are able to grasp the subtleties of complex moral and ethical questions, such as those relating to war and environmental issues, and they will defend their viewpoints with fervor and cogency.
understand reasoning with regard to what's fair and what isn't.	will emphasize and debate fairness of a situation.

A gifted fifth-grader argues passionately for the right of Dr. Kevorkian to continue his attendance at suicides. "It's the absolute right of the patient to decide his own fate," she says. A sixth-grade student is equally persuasive in presenting the case for gifted programs in elementary schools. "It's important for our psychological development," she says, "for us to spend time with other students who are like us." These philosophical statements are not what one expects from the average ten- and eleven-year-old child.

But having an advanced intellectual understanding of morals and ethics doesn't necessarily make gifted children more ethical than their classmates in day-to-day activities. Gifted children are children first; they can fib and evade responsibility just like any other child, usually more cleverly and with greater originality. There are a couple of reasons for this disparity:

- The child's experience hasn't yet caught up with his intellectual development; the child is not mature enough to understand that concern with moral issues must be translated into action in concrete situations.
- Gifted children, like others, want to be liked and to have friends. They get tired of standing out, of being a minority. The need for peer acceptance becomes very strong when they reach their teens, and they may

veer away from their personal moral compass or compromise their standards to gain a place with peers in the larger group.

For example, a student who dislikes heavy metal music and is opposed to the kind of conduct that is often part of the concert scene may nonetheless attend rock concerts and indulge in some possibly dangerous behaviors, such as "moshing," just to be part of a particular peer group.

Self-Image	
Smart Children:	**Gifted Children:**
share interests with peers and "fit in" at school; they tend to think that others like them, and thus develop high self-esteem.	generally have high self-esteem, but some may feel different from others, may not "fit in," and so may develop low self-esteem.
strive, achieve, and enjoy their accomplishments.	express dissatisfaction with their performance, because "there's so much more to do" or "I just didn't do it right."
seldom worry about being perfect.	can be intensely self-critical and perfectionistic.

Judyth, an elementary school student, mastered a group of very complex poems for presentation to a large group of parents and students. Her delivery, timing, and interpretation were flawless. After watching the videotape of her presentation, however, this highly gifted student was terribly embarrassed and said, "Oh, my face was so red!" Her focus was drawn to the one thing she saw as "wrong" with her performance, rather than to the overall excellence of her work. She actually believed she had done poorly.

These charts show that although both gifted children and smart children like to learn, work hard, and value friendships, gifted children show these traits with greater intensity.

In determining whether a child is gifted, *an important thing to look for is the degree to which specific traits are displayed.* The difference between a smart child and a gifted child often lies in the depth and intensity of these traits. For example, almost every child is curious. Smart children are probably more curious than average children, but gifted children are usually voraciously curious. They have a greater depth and intensity of curiosity.

Perhaps language is the issue. Whereas a smart child will be able to converse intelligently, a gifted child will often be able to converse and comprehend like an adult. Gifted children have a quicker grasp of language and can use it much more effectively than other children.

This intensity, which is sometimes referred to as "overexcitability," is a particularly important clue that parents and teachers can use to help them determine whether a child is smart or gifted. Later on, the child probably will be tested to determine more precisely the level and type of giftedness, but in the beginning, watch for intensity.

If your child is smart, but not gifted, some experts feel you might actually be fortunate. Leta Hollingworth, a noted pioneer in the gifted education field, described a concept of "optimal intelligence" which she said is probably between 120 and 145 IQ. As James Webb, clinical psychologist and one of the authors of *Guiding the Gifted Child: A Practical Source for Parents and Teachers*,[7] often tells parents, "The lower part of optimal intelligence isn't in the gifted range. Giftedness in most school districts begins at 130 IQ, and scores can go beyond 200 IQ. The good news is that with optimal intelligence, your child can succeed at just about anything occupationally. The bad news is that you'd better start putting away money for college."

If a child has been identified through psychological testing or group ability tests as gifted, you may be pleased, but at the same time prepare yourself for the ups and downs of parenting and teaching a challenging child. Read and learn all you can about the academic, social, and emotional characteristics and needs of these special children; then hang on for the ride.

---

[7]Webb, J. T., Meckstroth, E. A., & Tolan, S .S. (1982). *Guiding the gifted child: A practical source for parents and teachers*. Dayton, OH: Ohio Psychology Press (now Gifted Psychology Press).

Parents and teachers of a gifted child are in the best position to be the child's advocates. It's critical that these adults serve as advocates and mentors, because much of society is unaware of the special needs of gifted children. People without training in the characteristics of gifted children may be quick to judge and criticize children they don't understand. Gifted children need adults to support them when they feel confused, friendless, and frightened.

If you need professional help to understand and guide your child, don't hesitate to get it. Contact your local or state organization on gifted and talented to find the right resources. Many of these organizations and other resources are listed in the appendix at the end of this book. Although one person, often a parent or teacher, can make all the difference in a gifted child's life, it's possible that these important adults may need some advice and counsel along the way. Seeking help from various professionals, talking it out with other parents or teachers, or finding additional mentors for your child aren't signs that you're a weak or incompetent parent. These actions show that you're an adult who cares about what's best for these unusual children.

Section Two

Your Gifted Child and the School

Chapter 3

Testing and Screening: How Schools Identify Giftedness

If you've observed your child over a period of time and have come to the conclusion that he might be gifted, you are about to embark on a journey fraught with thrills, chills, spills, and wills. A mother recently shared that her child's pediatrician had made the "diagnosis" of giftedness and explained that the parents would now be placed in the position of advocating for their son throughout his entire elementary and secondary school career. "Schools aren't set up to handle children like yours," he said, "and society won't reward him much, either, at least until he's older."

The doctor is both right and wrong. In some school systems or individual school buildings within a school district, administrators and teachers agree on the importance of educating *all* children appropriately and make the accommodations necessary to serve gifted children. However, there are still many districts and schools in this country and others where the child is expected to lockstep through the regular curriculum, with little or no academic adjustment being made. That's why, in many parts of the United States, parents are working actively with state associations for the gifted and legislative bodies to enact mandates that will require schools to provide the same type of care and special attention to gifted students as they do for less able students and those with disabilities. Whatever the situation in your school or district, if you are the parent of a gifted child, you may need to be heavily involved in your child's education and with the teachers, counselors, and administrators who direct and influence that education.

To give your gifted student the best possible environment for learning, you will have to try hard to understand and appreciate the viewpoints of your child's teachers, because you will need to communicate and work with a variety of them from the time your child is identified until she goes off to college.

The parent/teacher partnership most often begins with a discussion of the child's ability and performance, followed by a testing process. Usually, the parents, the teacher—or both—have noticed that the student has demonstrated some exceptional abilities and feel that investigating the need for specialized education may be warranted.

Depending on the school system, nomination or referral for testing for a gifted program can come from teachers; parents; community representatives, such as members of the clergy, scout leaders, volunteer coordinators, team coaches; or other adults with whom your child interacts on a regular basis, or from the children themselves.

If you wish to nominate your child to be considered for a gifted program, the words you use with her classroom teacher are important. A collaborative approach is the most useful one. It's not a good idea to barge into the classroom waving an article on giftedness or a test score saying, "My child is more intelligent than anyone else in the class. What are you going to do about it?"

It's far better to share specific observations with the classroom teacher with such statements as, "I've noticed some things about Jacqui that make me think she might have some academic differences from other children. As a first-grader, she read all of the *Little House on the Prairie* books, and now, as a second-grader, she reads and comprehends far above her grade level. The other day, she asked me how to divide one-eighth by one-third, so I think she's ahead in math as well. Have you seen anything similar? What do you think we should do to make sure she continues to progress?"

The teacher may agree or disagree with a parent's appraisal of the child's ability. If there's disagreement, it's time for parents and teacher to listen carefully to one another's observations and try to come to some resolution. But even if the teacher agrees whole-heartedly with a parent's views, a child's entry into a gifted program isn't automatic.

If there is a gifted program, the child must meet the school district criteria, which may include taking one or more tests. Certainly, a child is more than a test score, but tests can provide some objective ways of measuring ability and potential as well as achievement in various areas. Although the tests listed below are some of the ones school districts commonly use for identification of gifted children, there are many other types of tests. Individual tests are most often administered by a school psychologist or a clinical psychologist; group tests can be given by a trained teacher or counselor. Although not every school system uses tests to identify gifted children, it is helpful to know a little about the various tests that may be used. Additional information about such tests can be obtained from the manuals that accompany each test.

The Kinds of Tests Your Child May Take

Ability tests measure general intelligence, as well as such factors as language, memory, conceptual thinking, mathematical reasoning, verbal and nonverbal reasoning, visual motor abilities, and social intelligence. Frequently used ability tests include, but are not limited to:

- Stanford-Binet Intelligence Scale (Binet–IV, or Form L-M)
- Wechsler Intelligence Scale for Children (WISC-III)

- Wechsler Preschool and Primary Scale of Intelligence–
  Revised (WPPSI-R)
- Woodcock-Johnson Tests of Cognitive Ability
- Kaufman Brief Intelligence Test (KBIT)
- Otis-Lennon School Ability Test
- SRA Primary Mental Abilities Test
- Cognitive Abilities Test
- Matrix Analogies Test
- Ross Test of Higher Cognitive Processes

Achievement tests measure skills in various curriculum areas—that is, what students have learned. A gifted child might be administered one or two of the following commonly used achievement tests:

- Comprehensive Test of Basic Skills
- Metropolitan Achievement Tests
- SRA Achievement Series
- California Achievement Test
- California Test of Basic Skills
- Woodcock-Johnson Tests of Achievement
- Iowa Tests of Basic Skills
- Stanford Achievement Test

Behavioral rating scales offer the classroom teacher an opportunity to assess traits such as the child's ability to interact with others and his academics, leadership, creativity, and motivation. These scales are important adjuncts to the standardized tests, but the teacher's input or a score on a single rating scale should not be the sole criterion for your child's inclusion in or exclusion from a gifted program.

There are checklists and inventories related to identifying *creativity*, but because there are so many facets to creativity, the administration of these instruments should be only a part of the process. Interviews, story-telling, and portfolios should be included in the identification of creative students, and in some cases, a panel of expert judges can help assess the child's creative potential. *The Torrance Tests of Creative Thinking* are among the most commonly used standardized instruments for measuring creativity. Creativity competitions, such as *Destination ImagiNation* and *Future Problem Solving*, also provide opportunities for students to demonstrate their creativity.[8]

Children who are gifted in the *visual and performing arts* demonstrate those skills with each piece of artwork or performance, but there are screening tests as well, such as the *Seashore Measures of Musical Talents* and the *Meier Art Tests*, though they are rarely used.

The Leadership Skills Inventory can be used with children in grades six through twelve to assess their strengths in the nine skills necessary for *leadership development*: fundamentals of leadership, written communication, speech communication, character-building, decision-making, group dynamics, problem-solving, personal skills, and planning skills. However, observation of the student within and beyond the classroom is probably better than trying to measure leadership on an objective scale or test.

Most school personnel recognize that acceptance into a gifted program should be based on a multi-factored screening of many areas of the child's functioning. Test scores are part of this screening process, but other factors frequently considered include:

- nomination for a gifted program by teachers, parents, peers, teachers, psychologists, or counselors.
- teachers' reports of how well the student functions intellectually, socially, and emotionally.
- the student's motivation and preferred learning styles.
- the parents' interest in and support for their child's participation.
- the student's self-inventory of values, interests, and attitudes toward school and extracurricular activities.[9]

---

[8]Piirto, J. *Understanding those who create*, pp. 118-119, 130.
[9]Clark. *Growing up gifted*, pp. 281-285.

Those who have the authority to make placement recommendations gather all the information, both objective and subjective, discuss it in detail, and make the decision about whether the child will be admitted to the gifted program.

Test Bias

When a procedure favors any one group over another, it is said to have bias. The major problem with over-reliance on standardized testing as the primary criterion for inclusion in gifted programs is that many tests favor those who are fluent in English, particularly if the students are from privileged backgrounds. Yet we know that gifted students are found in every socio-economic group and among students with disabilities. *Test bias*, that is, test construction that mirrors the language and experience of middle-class white students, can exclude from gifted programs minorities, children from lower socio-economic brackets, recent immigrants, those with limited English proficiency, and children with various hearing, speech, vision, and/or learning impairments.

In some school districts, this problem is being addressed through the use of other types of test instruments, such as the *Krantz Talent Identification Instrument* and *Torrance's Creative Positives.* There are non-verbal tests, such as the *Naglieri Nonverbal Ability Test, Raven's Progressive Matrices Test,* and the *Universal Nonverbal Intelligence Test*, which do not rely heavily on language abilities. A few of the more widely used tests, such as the *Cognitive Abilities Test*, make special accommodations to meet the needs of students with disabilities and those who speak little English. Some tests, such as the *Leiter-R*, are available for students with speech, language, or hearing impairments. There are now tests written in other languages, such as *Aprenda: La Prueba de Logros en Español, Bateria-R Woodcock-Muñoz*, and the *Escala de Intelligencia Wechsler Para Niños, Revisada*.

Different states have approved various tests to determine giftedness; therefore, a test accepted in one state may not be approved in another. Your school district will have information on what tests, if any, your child will need to take.

Tests can give you a snapshot of your child's strengths, as well as areas that aren't so outstanding—and remember, gifted children probably will not excel in every area or subject. As a parent, you have the right to have test results explained to you.

Making Sure No Child Is Missed: Beyond Standardized Tests

A group of researchers at the National Research Center on the Gifted and Talented have identified ten core attributes of giftedness:

- communication skills
- creativity/imagination
- inquiry
- insight
- interest
- memory
- motivation
- problem solving
- reasoning

These professionals argue that a variety of techniques beyond paper and pencil tests should be used to see if economically disadvantaged students, who might otherwise be passed over for gifted programs, possess some of these attributes. They recommend checklists, interviews, and rating scales in addition to other tests.[10] Although these recommendations are especially helpful for disadvantaged children, many school districts use this type of approach for all students being assessed for inclusion in gifted programs.

---

[10]Frasier, M. M., Hunsaker, S. L., Lee, J., Mitchell, S., Cramond, B., Garcia, J. H., Martin, D., Frank, E., & Finley, V. S. (1995). *Core attributes of giftedness: A foundation for recognizing the gifted potential of economically disadvantaged students* (RM95210). Storrs, CT: The National Research Center on Gifted and Talented, University of Connecticut.

More and more frequently, portfolios of children's work are being included as part of the identification process. A portfolio is a selection of the student's work collected over time that demonstrates the child's intellectual growth and development during a specific period. It can contain samples of artwork, music, stories, poems, and independent study projects. Portfolio assessment allows students to demonstrate a range of abilities that are generally not measured by standardized tests. The California Association for the Gifted describes a further benefit of portfolios: they "more closely parallel what adults do in the 'real world' to exhibit the quality of their work."[11] Expert observers can also make judgments about the child's degree of creativity based on the creative products that have been selected for the portfolio.[12] Portfolios are, of course, necessary for assessing students who are gifted in visual and performing arts.

Multi-factored assessment is particularly important for a group of children one might expect would be easily identified—the highly gifted. Identification of these children can be difficult because, during the testing process, they often "hit the ceiling." Many standardized tests, especially group tests, do a poor job of truly measuring the abilities of highly gifted youngsters because the children score as high as the test will go (the ceiling), and that score may then be incorrectly interpreted as representing their true ability level. In fact, when a child "tops out" on a test, in most cases it's the test that's deficient. A child with an IQ of 165 will, of course, score 150 on an instrument whose ceiling is 150. If further testing is not pursued, this child probably will not be identified as highly gifted and therefore may never be challenged adequately in the classroom. More testing, using a different instrument with a higher ceiling, is required to provide accurate testing information and successful interventions.

Some school systems use a "try-out" screening process.[13] In this situation, a program for gifted learners is provided for all ele-

---

[11]California Association for the Gifted. (1998) The challenge of raising your gifted child. Mountain View, CA: California Association for the Gifted.

[12]Piirto, J. Understanding those who create, p. 119.

[13]Van Tassel-Baska, J. (1998). Disadvantaged learners with talent. In Van Tassel-Baska (Ed.), Excellence in educating gifted and talented learners, p. 98. Denver, CO: Love Publishing Company.

mentary students for a specific time period. A group of specially selected teachers observe the children, looking for general intelligence, conceptual thinking, highly developed language skills, various types of reasoning ability, and the ability to relate to others. Once the teachers have watched the children over a period of time, they present their findings to a selection committee. These findings, which have the potential to be somewhat subjective, are combined with objective data, such as test scores, checklists, inventories, and portfolios, to help identify students for the gifted program.

An Important Reason for Identifying All Gifted Children

For gifted programs to survive, the identification umbrella must be extended as far as possible. A minority administrator makes the point dramatically: "We can't continue to support what amounts to apartheid in gifted education. The United States is changing. In less than twenty years, as people of color achieve majority status, the current white majority will become a minority. If we continue to identify predominantly white, economically advantaged students for gifted programs, eventually there will be fewer and fewer of these children in proportion to the rest of the student body. With so few students, it will no longer be economically feasible to support this type of special education. So seeking out gifted minority students is the right thing to do economically as well as morally. It ensures that gifted programs will continue for *all* students."

About the Testing Process

All testing, individual or group, can put a child under stress. Individual tests can be stressful because they take at least an hour to administer, and the child is interacting one-to-one with an adult. Even though the adult will try to make the experience pleasant, that intense interaction may feel threatening to some children. Psychologists are trained to establish rapport with the child before beginning the test, however, and parents can be assured that the testing process will be halted if the child shows signs of unusual stress.

Group testing can bring its own set of stressors. Group scores are greatly affected by the environment in which the test is given. There is a possibility that the children will be distracted by intrusive noises, interruptions, or even by the presence of others. In addition, some high-ability students become very upset if they sense that another child is answering more quickly or with less difficulty. The pressure of the group itself may actually cause these children to perform poorly. In addition, group tests often favor children who read well. A near-genius child who isn't a great reader can falter on a test that depends on reading competence.

There's no such thing as a "pure" test. Individually or collectively, children can be influenced by the setting—the temperature of the room, what they had for breakfast, how well they slept the night before, family stresses such as a move or parental separation, and other considerations. If you've had your child tested before and the numbers are slightly different this time, you probably can chalk it up to test conditions. You might even want to inquire about having the child retested.

When you request that the school system test your child, it's your right—and also your responsibility—to communicate any factors that might have an impact on the testing process. No state allows individual testing of students without a parent's consent, but once you've given your permission in writing, the school may schedule the test whenever the psychologist or other test administrator is available. Sometimes that may not be the best time for your child. If there are conditions school personnel should know about, make them known at the time you give permission.

Perhaps, for example, your son has serious allergies to spring grasses and flowers and has to take medication at that time of year. You're within your rights to ask that testing take place in the fall, when the child is not medicated. You are also within your rights to request that the school notify you a day or two in advance of the testing; perhaps there are some encouraging words you'd like to say to your daughter before she goes to take the test.

The point is, communicate up front. It's unfair to blame school officials for testing your child without informing you if you didn't ask to be informed. Don't criticize and complain about the incompetent people at the elementary school who tested your child on the very day the flowering trees burst into bloom if you never let the testers know about his allergies.

There are a few exceptions to this rule. You may have to communicate after the testing if the test took place at 10:00 a.m., and Yasmin left school with a temperature of 104° at noon. If she was becoming ill during the test, it's likely she might not have done as well as she would under other circumstances. These occasions are rare, however. If it's important enough for you to have the child tested in the first place, it should be a priority to bring any concerns to the tester before the test is administered. And because gifted children are sensitive souls, discuss these issues privately, out of the child's hearing, or in writing. However, later you will likely want to talk, at least in general, with your child about the testing process, as well as about what the testing suggested.

It's not necessary to have your child tested the moment she springs from the womb. Remember that very young students who come from homes where there is lots of enrichment will probably score higher than those with less exposure to reading, language, books, and conversation. Scores may fall slightly as the children grow—a part of the "leveling out" process. You can do your smart child a great disservice by insisting on a gifted placement before intellectual competencies sort themselves out. However, in the case of a child you suspect is highly gifted, early testing might be essential to qualify her for early entrance to school or into a gifted program.

Exceptional circumstances, such as evidence of profound giftedness or tantrums that appear to be intelligence-related, may justify earlier testing, but in general, it's best to let little children be little children, to let them bang the pots and spoons and explore the world the way little children do. According to Nancy Robinson,

"Psychological testing is advised only in special circumstances; parents can, in fact, describe their children's development rather accurately."[14] In other words, unless you have a clear reason to get a professional opinion during your child's earliest years, your own observations about his gifts, talents, and interests usually will suffice. By the end of first grade or the beginning of second, if you're picking up some clues you think the schools are missing, it might be time to raise the issue of testing with the child's teacher.

Parents sometimes choose to have their children tested privately. That's an acceptable option. Be aware, however, that even though school personnel may be required by law to accept, abide by, and make decisions based on scores from an outside source, some of them may more readily accept testing conducted by a school-recommended psychologist than testing conducted by an unknown specialist. The school staff know the school psychologists and how they carry out the testing procedure.

Nonetheless, very few school psychologists are experts in the needs of gifted children, and frankly, some of them are not trained to work with this group of students at all. If you have special concerns, you can take your child to an outside psychologist for testing. It may be well worth the cost to know the results, and it will provide you with a written record that often is far more extensive and detailed than the report the school will provide.

Before you have your child tested, either privately or by the school, ask yourself why you're having it done. For some parents, it's a matter of great importance. They suspect giftedness and want to have it confirmed so they can take the steps necessary to help their child excel and be happy. Other parents are just curious about what is appropriate to expect of their children. If you're one of these curious parents and you have the time and money to spend for testing—and if the child thinks testing might be fun or interesting—there's probably no harm in getting testing done.

Don't test for reasons such as bragging rights at the family reunion, however. If you're testing to satisfy your own ego, think twice (or even three times) before you put your child through it.

[14]Robinson, N. M. (1993). *Parenting the very young, gifted child* (RBDM9308). Storrs, CT: The National Research Center on the Gifted and Talented, University of Connecticut.

Before Testing

Please don't try to "prep" your child for the tests. A truly gifted child doesn't need preparation, and by placing such great emphasis on the test procedures and results, you're creating unnecessary stress for the child. Since gifted children usually already want very much to excel, parental cram sessions can be detrimental. They can give the child the sense that all the parents' hopes and dreams are riding on this set of tests, which is just not fair. How would you perform under such circumstances?

If you really want to provide optimal conditions for testing, give your child a good breakfast and a big smile, and tell him to have fun. Trust the child to do the best possible job on the test. It's out of your hands, so you may as well stop fretting about it.

The Best Thing You Can Do ...

... is to relax—especially regarding your child's IQ score. Intelligence is multi-dimensional; an IQ score does not measure everything about giftedness and is only one measure that summarizes a complex set of abilities. Your child's test scores are neither a positive nor a negative reflection on you as a parent. Your child is an individual with her own strengths and weaknesses. You really can't take the credit—or the blame—for her test performance.

If you are certain, for example, that your child falls into the gifted category, but the test scores fail to validate your perception, your child is still your child—bright, capable, lovable, and probably still in the "optimal range" of intelligence. If you show disappointment in the child's test performance, what kind of message are you sending? Tell the child that you're sure she did well, and that you know she is bright, competent, and able to accomplish great things.

If your child does test in the gifted range, that's great. But don't get too carried away. Giftedness doesn't guarantee a free, smooth ride through school or through life. You have a long and sometimes bumpy road ahead, just like every other parent, and you will likely be heavily involved in your child's education from the day of identification to the day of graduation.

Chapter 4

Parents and Teachers: Understanding One Another

The best school situation for any student, gifted or not, is a classroom where he feels safe and valued and where achievement is expected and encouraged. Children feel *safe* when they know that there are supportive classroom limits, that behaviors—positive or negative—result in consistent consequences, and that they will not be publicly punished or privately humiliated. Students feel *valued* and motivated to achieve when adults listen to them, allow them to explore, give them a voice in planning classroom activities, reward them when they try things that stretch their intellectual limits, and respect their dignity and individuality.

Those are the "givens." But when you're looking for a school for your gifted child, what specific indicators tell you whether or not he is likely to thrive there? One way to learn is to view teachers in action, but there's a right way and a wrong way to go about asking permission to observe teachers' classrooms.

Some Inside Information about Teachers

When you're at work, what's it like when your supervisor stands over you, evaluating and criticizing your work? Are you on edge? Tense? Do you feel less competent than you know you are? That's exactly how a teacher feels when parents he or she doesn't know suddenly ask if they can come into the classroom to determine whether that teacher is "suitable" for their child.

Being a teacher has always been difficult, but perhaps never more so than today. It's understandable that teachers might be less than welcoming to parents who act as if they have come in to condemn the teacher's classroom management techniques and find fault with her teaching abilities. Unfortunately, that's how some parents present themselves, and that critical attitude sets the stage for confrontation, not cooperation.

You have the right to observe a classroom, but a better way to gather the information you need is from being in the school as a friend of teachers and an advocate for education. Take the time to make yourself known around the school. Go to parents' nights, attend school fund-raisers, and participate in parent activities.

If you're a working parent and can't volunteer in the library or work on the school newsletter, find other ways to become involved. Be the courier who picks up and returns the public library materials the teacher is using for a particular unit. Sign up to be an usher for a school function. Make a batch of your famous cookies for the bake sale. Guide visitors on parents' night. Offer to be a computer tutor one evening a week. Help your child's teacher with a special project. Participate in the work group that builds the new playground or paints the classroom.

Parents often have special knowledge, talents, or skills that would enrich the classroom. They may be fluent in another language, be artistic, know how to cook ethnic food, or play an instrument. All of these skills could be shared with students. Sometimes teachers need someone to listen to students read or to supervise a study group. Parents who are properly trained might lead book discussion groups or help students with *Future Problem Solving* or

Destination ImagiNation academic competitions. There are literally hundreds of ways to inject yourself into the school environment, no matter how busy your schedule. All parents have something to give.

Once you're known as a participative parent and a team player, it's easier to approach a teacher, share your questions about your child, and have a meaningful discussion about those issues. If teachers see you as a concerned parent and a partner in education, if they know that your emphasis is on doing what's best for your child, not on criticizing the school and the faculty, their attitude will be much more open and welcoming. They will be more willing to provide information about the best academic placement for your child now and in the future. Facts gathered this way are more reliable than impressions gained from stilted, formal, evaluative classroom observations.

Being active in the schools is part of a long-term strategy for getting your child's needs met, because helping him navigate the educational establishment isn't something you do once; it's an ongoing activity, from the elementary grades through high school graduation and beyond.

As the primary advocates for their child, parents must familiarize themselves with the kinds of teaching and learning activities used and supported in the child's school. They should find out if there are alternative programs available. They should be knowledgeable about the strengths and weaknesses of all the program options and be able to assess whether these options would be appropriate for their child. Parents can discover that information most effectively by being part of the school community. Once they know and trust you, administrators and teachers will be much more likely to respect your views and be frank about their opinions. They will be more inclined to treat you as an important part of the education team.

Be careful that the advocacy activities you carry out for your child are tempered with respect for the child's teacher and other representatives of the school. If you go in with a "know-it-all" attitude, you should not expect to get much cooperation.

The Parent/Teacher Partnership

Parents and teachers of gifted students face different challenges. Parents are constantly dealing with the social and emotional needs of their children, and the daily ups and downs can be exhausting.

Teachers experience your child's ups and downs, too, as well as the ups and downs of every other child in the class. Because teachers are expected to provide the most appropriate education for every child, some are simply overwhelmed. Your child's classroom may contain as many as twenty-five to thirty children with greatly varying needs: students with various handicapping conditions, children who have suffered abuse or have severe emotional problems, students just learning to speak English, and other children with special learning needs.

In addition, the elementary classroom teacher often is given the responsibility for repairing damaged self-esteem; offering substance abuse education; helping students learn about good touch, bad touch, and stranger danger; imparting character education (which used to be exclusively the parents' responsibility); and still teaching enough math, reading, and social studies content to enable students to pass state-mandated achievement and proficiency tests. In many schools, teachers also handle lunchroom and playground duty. Is it any wonder that the needs of gifted children are neglected? It's easy to see why teachers might be tempted to rationalize and say that gifted children will learn things on their own.

The best way to see that your child reaches his full potential is to form alliances with his teachers, because when it comes to dealing with these challenging, rewarding children, *parents and teachers are the strongest resources for one another*. They should turn to each other immediately if either of them suspects that a child is gifted or when an identified gifted child has difficulties. They need to check out their own perceptions against those of the other.

Parents sometimes hear things from educators that don't match their own instincts about their child. In these cases, remember that the child's teacher is coming from another perspective—a perspective formed by several hours of daily observation over a long period of time. His or her viewpoint will surely differ from yours.

Think about it this way: If you're standing at the base of a ninety-story skyscraper, it looks huge. You can't even see the top floors. View the same building from ten miles away, however, and you can cover its entire outline with your index finger. You have to combine both perspectives to arrive at a real judgment about the building's size.

It's the same with your gifted child. Both your perceptions and the teacher's probably are accurate, but when they are combined, only then do you get the total picture.

For example, Antwan, nine, has an amazingly long attention span at home. Does the teacher observe that trait, too? At school, Sally, eight, loves to write and has created her own multi-chapter books. Does she exhibit that gift for language at home? Carlos, ten, gets upset very easily if he doesn't receive a perfect score on his spelling tests. Is he always perfectionistic, or is he having difficulty only at school? When parents and teachers work together to construct a comprehensive picture of the whole child, they can make cooperative decisions about such issues as testing and curriculum adjustments with greater certainty and confidence.

Unfortunately, parents and teachers of gifted students all too often can view each other as adversaries. Teachers may believe that the parents are attacking their classroom methods, are pushing the gifted student, and are snobbish know-it-alls. Conversely, they may believe that the parents aren't doing enough to encourage their child's special gifts. Parents may think that the teacher is some sort of drone who doesn't appreciate their child's giftedness, or on the other hand, that she picks on the child and is far too demanding.

Jim and Sue Ellen are the parents of Kyle, a gifted six-year-old. Kyle's initial first-grade report is substandard, at least in his parents' eyes. They expected that Kyle would go immediately into the top group in every area and are appalled to discover he's not even in accelerated reading. They wonder about his teacher. Is she knowledgeable about the needs of gifted children?

Kyle's parents need to refrain from jumping to conclusions about what's going on in the classroom. Instead, they should make an appointment with Kyle's teacher and share their concerns directly with her, keeping the focus on the child, not on their perceptions of the teacher's capabilities (or lack of them). They might be pleasantly surprised to hear, "I'm glad you came in. Kyle *is* extremely capable, but, as you know, sometimes these kinds of students go through periods where they need a bit more emotional support. That's how it's been with Kyle. I thought it was important to get him comfortable with his surroundings and with the other children before I moved him into accelerated reading. He'll be in that group within a week or two." In this case, the teacher is well aware of Kyle's capabilities and has his best interests at heart.

On the other hand, Kyle's teacher might be exasperated by what she perceives as his inattentiveness during her lessons. By questioning the parents, she may learn from them, "Oh, that's just Kyle. We're never sure if he hears us either, but when we talk to him later, we find that he remembers what we said. He just seems to have a lot going on in his head." By listening to Kyle's parents, the teacher has gained some valuable insights.

What's important is for parents and teachers to share information, not prejudices. By combining their observations, rather than protecting their separate spheres, teachers and parents can learn to trust one another and do what's best for the child. Then, even if disagreements should arise, they will have built a solid framework of respect that will serve them well as they resolve issues together.

If the school system is fortunate enough to have a gifted education specialist, it's very important that he or she be involved in the communication with parents as well. The specialist is a vital link between the classroom teacher and the parents, available to both at all times. This invaluable resource person has had extensive training in and a clear understanding of the academic, social, and emotional needs of gifted students; the specialist can offer both daily and long-term guidance to teachers and parents as they deal with the many complex issues surrounding giftedness. In addition, should there be a disagreement between teacher and parents, the gifted education specialist is in the ideal position to offer neutral advice and inventive solutions.

For the good of the child, both parents and teachers need to rein in their own biases, work together as equals, and keep the lines of communication between home and school open and humming.

Who Should Teach Your Gifted Child?

It's a rare school that allows parents to request specific teachers for individual students; in general, school administrators fear that chaos would erupt if all parents were permitted to select their children's teachers. There's no harm in trying to place your child with a particular teacher, however, if you have substantive reasons and sufficient evidence that the placement would be advantageous for your child. Support for such a request could include a recommendation from the prior year's teacher, the gifted education coordinator, or a Child Study Team, if there is one. Try to negotiate reasonably rather than make noisy demands if you want to increase your chances for success.

Joyce Van Tassel-Baska mentions several characteristics necessary for teachers if they are to be effective with gifted learners. They include: (1) eager backing of acceleration options for able learners, (2) the capability to modify a curriculum, (3) adequate training and competence in the content area, and (4) preparation in organizing and managing classroom activities.[15] Barbara Clark states that teachers of the gifted should have an "uncommon ability" to empathize with and inspire students; share enthusiasm, a love of learning, and a joy of living; be authentic and humane; be alert, knowledgeable, and informed; tolerate ambiguity; and value intelligence, intuition, diversity, uniqueness, change, growth, and self-actualization.[16] Gifted students say they want their teachers to

---

[15]Van Tassel-Baska, J. (1991). Identification of candidates for acceleration: Issues and concerns. In *The academic acceleration of gifted children* (Southern and Jones, Eds). NY: Teachers College Press.
[16]Clark. *Growing up gifted*, p. 226.

understand them, exhibit a sense of humor, make learning fun, and be cheerful.[17] What's not important is the teacher's age, race, ethnicity, or gender.

Useful Traits in Working with Gifted Children

Facilitating attitude and behavior

When it comes to gifted children, teachers are not endless sources of knowledge, but facilitators, guiding and channeling the child's creativity and inventiveness. The teacher must know how to help the child learn and be able to point him in the direction of the resources—printed, electronic, and human—that can best broaden his intellectual, social, and emotional horizons.

Additionally, the teacher must be committed to truth and fairness. Because gifted children are so attuned to justice and honesty, the teacher must model these attributes without fail.

Finally, the teacher's attitude should reflect acceptance of diversity. She should believe in the potential of children of every race and ethnic group and be aware of the ways in which giftedness is expressed in various cultures.

Self-confidence

A teacher of gifted children must have enough self-assurance not to be rattled when a student knows more than the teacher about a particular subject. When gifted students get excited about topics, they are capable of deep and thorough research and can quickly become experts on some pretty esoteric material. No teacher should be expected to know everything about every topic that might catch

---

[17]Kathnelson, A. & Colley, L. (1982). *Personal and professional characteristics valued in teachers of the gifted.* Paper presented at California State University. Los Angeles, CA.

a gifted child's fancy. He should take delight in the student's interests, not feel threatened by them.

Resourcefulness and flexibility

Because they are often restricted by budget constraints, good teachers know how to use everything—from toilet paper tubes to tree bark to kitchen funnels to playing cards—as learning materials. Your child's teacher should be creative enough to see the educational potential in nearly everything, and the room should be full of all kinds of things children can use to learn. In addition, the teacher should have lots of strategies at her disposal, so that if one idea doesn't work, another teaching method is ready for immediate use.

Creativity and open-mindedness

Gifted children sometimes solve problems in unusual ways. The teacher shouldn't be locked into a "best way," or worse, "the only way" to arrive at the answer to a question or problem, but instead should understand and applaud the gifted student's ingenuity. It's ingenuity, after all, that untangles life's big issues and wins Nobel Prizes and MacArthur "Genius" Grants. A teacher shouldn't be afraid of it.

Trusting attitude

The teacher should never relinquish his authority, but must not be overly anxious when the student is working independently. The teacher has to exhibit confidence that the student is capable of working alone until the child demonstrates otherwise.

Cultural knowledge

Gifted children often have passionate interests in music, theater, or dance. The teacher should be knowledgeable enough about these subjects to be comfortable discussing them and should know how to use the arts as part of the educational process. A Shakespearean play, for example, is more than a piece of theater; it's a window into a historical period, and the teacher should be able to exploit this exciting resource to extract all the learning possible, not only about the play, but also about its historical and social context. A teacher whose students include a number of different ethnicities should be willing to explore her students' cultures—from food to poetry to music and dance.

Technical knowledge

The teacher doesn't need to know everything there is to know about computer programming or wireless communication, but he must be able to guide students in using all sorts of technological tools, including the World Wide Web.

Imagine children's excitement about being part of a multinational Internet research group of similarly talented students, perhaps led by an internationally renowned expert. Not only will the students gain significant educational benefits, but they'll also discover that they're not alone in the world. They can find other students in various parts of the world with the same interests, gifts, and challenges. That discovery can go a long way in helping gifted children feel less isolated and out of place.

Stamina

Gifted students, like other students with special educational needs, take a lot out of a teacher. She must have the ability to keep up with the children's high energy level and constant questioning.

The teacher also must have an almost limitless ability to listen. Listening to a gifted child all day can zap anyone's endurance. But listening is critical. A gifted child often needs to try out ideas by talking about them, seemingly *ad infinitum*, and the teacher must be able to listen, direct, redirect, and respond appropriately. That takes stamina.

The teacher must possess a tolerance for students with high levels of curiosity, for independent and creative thought, and for frequent challenges to the existing ways of doing things.

Subject matter competence and skill

Teachers who have the ability to practice what they teach are especially helpful to gifted children. A music teacher who is a practicing musician, an art teacher who has participated in exhibits, a language arts teacher who publishes short stories or poems, a science teacher who actively researches her own areas of interest, or a psychology teacher who volunteers at a crisis center all model the potential, application, and importance of what they teach. These teachers do not rely solely on textbooks, handouts, or other curricular materials; they bring their experience and creativity to the classroom.

Sense of humor

In the high-stress occupation of teaching gifted children, the ability to laugh with—not at—them is essential. And the teacher should be prepared to laugh at himself, too. Jokes, wordplay, and various types of humor that might be too sophisticated for average students are often highly enjoyable for gifted children, and a light touch can go a long way in helping students who are sometimes tense and perfectionistic.

Real interest in and love for these unusual students

A teacher should not view gifted children as a burden, but as a wonderful opportunity to stretch, to learn, and to grow professionally. She must be committed to constant continuing education to learn to appreciate and accommodate the diversity of each child's particular talents and gifts.

Chapter 5

Helping Gifted Children Learn

You may have an idea of the kind of teacher you want your child to have, but what sort of classroom environment and curriculum will best meet her needs?

The Ideal Classroom

Let's imagine you've decided to visit your child's classroom to see if you think it works for him. The ideal classroom is more than an assortment of desks and chairs and bulletin boards. It's a place of learning and discovery where children are invited to participate with spirit and imagination.

The ideal classroom is connected to the environment. It's a place where teachers open children's minds to the magic and charm of the world around them. If a child catches a butterfly on the way to school, the classroom should have a place for that butterfly—a place where the child can see it, watch it, study it, and enjoy its beauty.

The ideal classroom is geared to the various ways children learn. Students learn through their eyes, ears, hands, mouths, and noses. They learn in groups and alone. They learn through the use of music, art, and nature, as well as from textbooks and other resources, and the room should accommodate a variety of learning styles, including visual, auditory, kinesthetic, and others.

Have you ever looked into a classroom and seen alphabet charts hung above the chalkboard? Those charts should instead be at the children's eye level, so students can look at the letters, trace them with their fingers or even with tracing paper, and see, up-close, the relationships between B and P or C and O.

The ideal classroom will be filled with samples of student-made products and will be arranged with nooks, crannies, and corners left open for independent projects and supplies. The room might even look a little messy because of all the "stuff" the students are in the process of making. Bulletin boards will not be perfect, but instead will show traces of smudgy little fingerprints that attest to the fact that the children created part of the visual environment of their classroom.

The ideal classroom will change with the developmental needs of the children. The teacher will not hold preconceived notions about every detail of classroom arrangement and decor, but will be open to the children's suggestions and ideas. Building such an environment is a bit like knitting a scarf with left-over strands of yarn; you're not sure exactly what the finished product will look like, but you know it will be colorful and keep you warm.

The classroom in which your child will gain greatest bene-fit is a place where she feels connected to the teacher, the other students, and learning. It is always changing, because learning takes place in the classroom, goes home with the students, is shaped by real-life experiences, and comes back to school in a dif-ferent form the next day. "Teachable moments" arise in the to and fro of children's lives, and the classroom needs to support those moments.

Some of these things are intangibles. But what else will you see on your visit to an ideal classroom?

You'll see students who are continually involved, and they'll be able to tell you not only what they're doing, but why. You won't witness chaos, but the room won't be silent, either. There will be an almost rhythmic pulsation of children actively involved in learning, moving around the classroom, working together or independently. You'll observe that the teacher and students are mutually arriving at decisions and plans, and you'll watch one-to-one communication between the teacher and individual students. You'll see some whole-class instruction and some small group work. If students have completed required work, you may notice them working on independent projects.

A classroom model familiar to many parents and teachers is one with several "learning centers" or "activity stations" for different types of student work. Teachers use learning centers in many different ways. Sometimes the centers are subject driven, as when there is an art center, a music center, a reading and writing center, and a science center. Other times, centers are built around the ways students learn. For students who learn best through language, there are centers with books, puppets, phonics cards, cassette recorders, word games, and other kinds of reading and language tools. Some centers contain hands-on equipment, such as puzzles, workshop or kitchen tools, and other materials for children who learn best by manipulating things. Another center might offer materials that appeal to children who learn best visually; these children grasp concepts more quickly through the use of various art media, videotapes, pictures, charts, and photographs. Learning centers can be quiet or hives of activity; sometimes there is only one student at a center and sometimes there are several students working together on a project.

The ideal classroom is student-friendly. This doesn't mean that the teacher abandons control and the children are free to do whatever they wish. A student-friendly classroom is one where the needs of each child drive decisions about classroom procedures. The teacher uses a variety of teaching methods—from lectures to media demonstrations to real-world activities to simulations—to make sure that all of the children's different learning styles are addressed. The teacher is the learning coach.

The ideal classroom will also feature *individualized instruction*, or teaching that matches students' ability levels. For many teachers, the optimal way to individualize instruction for all children is to group students together according to their abilities in math and reading. For social studies and science, students work on a general theme, but individual students and small groups may investigate interest areas related to the theme.

Opening the Umbrella: An Expanded Curriculum for the Gifted Student

Individualized instruction, with enrichment activities for high-ability students, works very well for the majority of class members. For the gifted, however, it's not enough. These students will be most challenged and will derive amazing benefits from an *expanded curriculum.*

An expanded curriculum is *not* one in which gifted students are simply given more of the same kind of work to keep them busy. (This is sometimes called the MOTS approach, which stands for "More Of The Same.") What's the point of giving a student who demonstrates complete mastery of a concept the "opportunity" to do six more worksheets of the same kind? Loading gifted children up with busy work almost guarantees passive withdrawal or disruptive, perhaps aggressive, behavior brought about by boredom and frustration.

To visualize the concept of an expanded curriculum, imagine a rainy day on which the teacher and students are going for a walk in the woods to look for rainbows. As they walk, the teacher holds a huge golf umbrella over the students' heads to protect them from the pelting rain. The majority of students are wearing yellow slickers, yellow rain hats, and yellow boots, and they remain with the teacher under the umbrella as they walk.

Some of the children, however, are wearing different colors of fluorescent rain gear. Chandra's slicker is green, José is in red, Stephanie sports a blue slicker, and Jason one that's orange. They've donned these different colored slickers because the teacher is going to allow them to venture out from under the umbrella to explore their areas of interest or talent, and the bright colors will keep them in sight as they wander away from the confines of the teacher's large umbrella. Although they have substantial freedom, the teacher can always see these students, and they remain under her supervision.

Prior to this walk in the woods, the teacher has worked with the gifted students to determine what areas they'd like to research, and she will provide additional guidance for them when they return to the classroom with the results of their explorations.

As the walk continues, Chandra darts out from the umbrella to indulge her fascination with science. She collects algae from the pond and saves it to take home to study under the little microscope her dad bought her for her birthday. José dashes away to study the cloud formations that drift along overhead. He's very interested in weather and how it affects the earth. Stephanie leaves the protection of the umbrella to sit under a rock outcropping, sheltered from the rain. She makes herself comfortable with a book of poetry. She loves to read the Romantic poets and comprehends the ideas and concepts behind their poems. Jason sits next to her; he writes his own versions of the poems as Stephanie reads them aloud. They're gone a long time, because they are busy sharing their thoughts.

When it's time to leave the woods, the teacher calls everyone together again. On their return to the classroom, she asks how many students saw a rainbow. She's thrilled that even those who never left her umbrella saw at least one. Jason, Stephanie, José, and Chandra saw a few additional things, however, because they were allowed to be outside the umbrella, looking in many different directions. They are now able to tell their classmates about what they saw from a variety of perspectives.

Back in the classroom, Chandra explains about prisms and the color spectrum, José discusses the weather conditions that have to be present for a rainbow to occur, Stephanie demonstrates the symbolism of rainbows in certain poems, and Jason reads an amusing story he wrote about a rainbow and a pig. After they have finished their presentations, these students further expand their research: Chandra spends more time in the science center; José visits with a meteorologist at a local television station; Stephanie revises some of her work; and Jason adds illustrations to his story and binds it so other students can check it out of the library.

In this individualized model, the teacher has provided all of the students with optimal learning, and the gifted students have experienced the joy of following their individual paths. The children have significant input into what they learn, but their independent study is carried out in the context of general themes the whole class is investigating. The gifted and talented children may choose their topics in conferences with the teacher or by filling out an interest inventory the teacher provides to arrive at specific topics for study.

To put it more concisely, a program for gifted children must provide pathways by which these students may venture away from the basic curriculum in areas in which they excel. This expansion of the curriculum may take place in their own classroom with guidance from the teacher; on field trips to museums, science centers, or cultural performances; or in a resource room that they go to on a regular basis where there is a teacher with special training—a gifted education specialist. The students come back to work with their other classmates when it's appropriate for them to do so, but do not necessarily do all of the same work that the other students are doing. Because the curriculum in some areas can be made shorter for gifted children, it allows them time for flexibility in other areas. Some gifted students will be "outside the umbrella" in every subject, others in only one or two. In all cases, the teacher or a teacher working with a gifted specialist creates the strategies that differentiate (modify) the curriculum to make fit the needs and learning styles of gifted students.

The goal of the expanded curriculum is to equip exceptional children for life. When teachers first encounter gifted students, it's clear that the children's analytical intelligence is highly developed; it's that kind of intelligence that makes them candidates for a gifted program in the first place. But life isn't about analytical intelligence, and gifted children are more than the sum of their test scores. They are human beings, and human beings don't spend their entire lives circling numbers and drawing analogies. They go through life meeting obstacles, encountering challenges, solving problems, and dealing with other people. The teacher's job is to act as diagnostician—to see where the children's gifts lie and then to provide relevant, authentic experiences through which they will develop what Yale psychologist Robert Sternberg calls their "tacit" knowledge—the skills that will someday allow them to use their giftedness in a wider context, such as an office, laboratory, classroom, or studio.

Psychologist B. F. Skinner once said, "Education is what survives after what has been learned has been forgotten." That's a pretty good definition of tacit knowledge. Tacit knowledge includes such skills as priority ranking, allocating time and resources, and managing oneself and others. When gifted children grow up, they need to be able to do such things as cook, work in conditions they might not like, socialize with others who may not be like them, and enjoy recreational pursuits. In the short term, they have to learn to make their beds, pick up their clothes, set the table, and take care of their pets.

Therefore, the ideal classroom for gifted students will balance open-ended, stimulating, and creative opportunities for divergent thinking and analysis with meaningful, practical activities that involve day-to-day living. If gifted students spend all their time in abstract reasoning and have no opportunities to exercise their gifts in realistic situations, they may never learn how to harness their strengths in ways that are satisfying to them and enable them to make a contribution to society. They will still be gifted, but their gifts might be underdeveloped or even lost. They might become discipline problems or lethargic underachievers. Or they might become behavior problems on a spectrum that ranges from occasionally acting out in class to ending up in the juvenile justice system.

Curriculum Differentiation: Too Hard To Do?

Differentiation for gifted students means providing learning options that meet the students' special needs for acceleration of content and greater depth, breadth, and complexity of instruction.

Some teachers think it's too difficult and time consuming to individualize daily lesson plans to accommodate these special students, but that's an inaccurate perception. It's actually easy to engage gifted children because they are open to so many different approaches and are excited about opportunities to accelerate or expand their learning in certain interest areas.

When a teacher provides ways for the gifted child to excel through small group investigation, independent study, or other options, he gains a valuable ally—the child. These students are so self-motivated that if they work together with their teacher to set goals and the teacher then gives them a gentle nudge in the right direction, the children take on much of the responsibility for their own learning. Naturally, the teacher supervises the students' activities, but teaching gifted children doesn't need to be an exercise in micro-management. When gifted children are fully engrossed, teachers find that they actually have more time to give to other students who need attention.

One third-grade teacher decided to differentiate her curriculum. "After several years in the field, I was tired of twenty-four pairs of eyes on me every day, awaiting my guidance in every subject all the time. I decided I had to try something different because I knew that many of my students weren't getting the most appropriate kind of help from me. The next year, I had two gifted students and several others who were very bright. The gifted students were good kids, but I was spending way too much time answering their constant questions and dealing with their interruptions. They monopolized every discussion, not because they wanted to, but because they knew the answers, and it was natural for them to want to move more quickly than the others. The average students weren't getting my best, and frankly, the gifted ones weren't either.

"I decided to put all of my students on contracts that made them responsible for a significant amount of their own learning. Because it was my first year to try contracts, I used them only in math, because progress in math is pretty easy to see. The contracts were very simple; the average students finished them slowly, but the gifted ones whizzed through them in a few days. I then met with these students, as well as some others who were progressing relatively rapidly. Over time, the gifted students' contracts became much more elaborate, with many more options for deeper, longer-term investigations. All the students in the class were learning about the same topics; they were just learning at the appropriate speed and level of complexity. The average students learned everything the standard curriculum required of them; the gifted students received that curriculum, too, but they were given additional challenges that were appropriate for their abilities and learning styles. Some of them just zoomed, tackling advanced topics such as probability theory.

"It worked so well in math that I added contracts for science in the second semester. By the next year, I was using learning centers and contracts very effectively, and all the students were doing well with them.

"The knowledge the children gained was important, but what was even more important was what happened to the atmosphere of the classroom. The gifted kids were so engaged and focused on their work that I could devote much more of my energy to the students who needed more hands-on assistance. Maybe they wanted some additional teacher-guided math practice or help with composition and spelling. The average students were much happier, the more able students were happier, the gifted students were happier, and I wasn't nearly so stressed out at the end of each day. I felt like a teacher, not a lion tamer. Learning centers and contracts are things I'll do for the rest of my career."

When children are engaged in appropriate learning, they channel energy that might otherwise be used in creating havoc in the classroom. When a teacher's time is spent primarily with two or three students, how much instruction do the others receive? Differentiating the curriculum is a win for teachers and a win for every student.

Finally, it's much harder to keep gifted children "under control" than it is to allow them to use their brains and energy to pursue subjects that arouse their interest and curiosity. To maintain a healthy learning environment, teachers need to have these children on their side. After all, how would you feel if you went into a classroom every day to learn and relearn things you had mastered three years before? Would you be happy and productive in that atmosphere? Wouldn't you begin to think of things you could do to make the class livelier?

The Perils of a Standard Curriculum

Meggie and Travis were two students who needed help to accommodate their special learning needs, but before those needs were met, they created a certain kind of chaos in the classroom.

Meggie was highly gifted and an exceptional artist; she was also the class clown, making jokes incessantly. Because her fourth-grade teacher was inexperienced in dealing with students like Meggie, she soon found herself on the losing end of a power struggle. The teacher responded to Meggie's acting out by becoming more and more strict. Meggie, in turn, became more and more frustrated and angry. Her parents tried to intervene and did everything they could at home, but the problems at school got worse.

Meggie's teacher had a policy that the children had to put their heads down on their desks after they came in from the noon recess. She felt it helped them calm down, collect their thoughts, and get ready for the afternoon. Meggie hated this enforced rest and carefully planned her strategy. One afternoon, when the class came in from the playground, Meggie put her feet up on her desk instead of lowering her head.

"Put your feet on the floor," her teacher said. Meggie refused. The teacher became irate. She said, "Meggie, I said put your feet on the floor. And I mean right now."

Meggie giggled and said, "Miss Caulfield, my feet are on the floor," and showed the class the perfect drawing she'd made of her bare feet—a drawing she'd placed carefully under her desk. At this, Miss Caulfield snapped and began yelling at Meggie that she wasn't funny, but her words were quickly drowned out by the laughter of the class. She had lost control of both herself and her classroom; she was stuck in a no-win situation. She felt she would never be able to regain the respect of her class after that incident.

After several discussions with the gifted resource teacher, Miss Caulfield came to realize that getting into power struggles with gifted children is useless. She learned that it's better to negotiate and allow some mutual decision-making so the children become your allies as well as your students. They can wield an enormous amount of influence over the other children, and you need their support. Gifted students are not always a teacher's delight, but it's the teacher's responsibility to find the strategies that work with them, just as she would for any other special needs child.

As a relatively new teacher, Miss Caulfield was very aware of her responsibilities to her students, but her conscientiousness sometimes made her classroom management style a little rigid. She made a carefully considered decision to relax her somewhat dictatorial rules, and she also entered into a contract with Meggie. She agreed to abolish the heads-down policy for a two-week trial period. The students would instead use this time to do silent reading or journaling. In exchange for this concession, Meggie would participate in the reading period without acting out or interrupting other students' work. During the two weeks, Miss Caulfield would determine whether the silent reading strategy was as effective as the rest period in getting the class ready for the remainder of the day. If it was, the heads-down policy would be abolished for good. Meggie agreed to the contract quickly because she liked writing and loved illustrating her journal. Suitably engaged, Meggie created far less uproar and Miss Caulfield became less tense. Because there was no overt power struggle between student and teacher anymore, the afternoons began to go much more smoothly. Rest period was no longer necessary.

Miss Caulfield also decided that she had taken many of Meggie's jokes and observations too personally, and she began to respond more positively to Meggie's humor. She maintained control of the classroom, but when one of Meggie's contributions resulted in a good laugh, Miss Caulfield went along with it and then got everyone back on track. Meggie blossomed in response to the change in the classroom style, and the other children were happier too.

Like Meggie, Travis was a discipline problem, but his issues were far more serious. Travis had been getting into trouble from his first day of kindergarten. He was disruptive on the school bus and threw stones at children and teachers on the playground. He was placed in a program for students with severe behavior handicaps, and by the time he reached the third grade, his file was an inch thick. At that point, the school psychologist tested Travis and found that his IQ was 160, placing him in the highly gifted category. However, the school principal refused to allow Travis to participate in the gifted education program until he shaped up his behavior in school. This decision was perhaps not surprising, but it's interesting to note that if Travis had had a hearing or vision handicap or an IQ significantly *below*, rather than *above*, the norm, he would have been admitted to a special program for students without question. He would not have been expected to change his behavior before he was placed in a program that met his special needs.

As a result of his growing frustration, Travis' behavior became even more extreme. Fortunately for him, a new principal was hired by the school, and she believed it was possible that Travis acted out aggressively due to frustration because the regular school curriculum did not match his ability. She immediately approved him for the gifted program.

Travis was part of the program for three years. During a sixth-grade project on the justice system, he learned what often happens to persons who use their gifts for negative purposes. It was an awakening for him. His behavior, which had been improving slowly, took a giant leap forward, and he became, if not a model school citizen, at least a student who stayed in class, rather than in detention or on suspension.

As Meggie and Travis illustrate, the standard school curriculum may actually be harmful to gifted children. If schools do not recognize this, then parents may need to become advocates for flexible educational options for their gifted children.

Parents as Teachers

It's impossible to overstate the importance of parents in the educational process, because parents are the child's first and most important teachers. They can expand the world for their children in ways a classroom teacher cannot.

Even if you're working and can't come to your child's school often, your workplace or home is full of learning opportunities. For example, let's say the teacher wants to take the students on a field trip to a local research institution. In the typical situation, the children and teacher receive the standard public tour and are hustled out the door. But if a parent works there, it's a whole new ball game. The red carpet is rolled out; students get to view areas not usually seen by the public; they eat in the cafeteria or commissary; they meet and talk with employees who are the parent's friends and hear about special projects the staff is working on. One of those conversations may light a fire between a student and a particular adult. That's a mentorship in the making. One parent's providing such a learning opportunity can affect many students' lives.

Living with a gifted child day in and day out gives parents insights into a child's world that even the most talented teacher can't discover. For instance, Jessie is very withdrawn and perfectionistic in class. In talking with Jessie's father, the teacher learns that Jessie talks often about the toy store she's going to open when she grows up. Jessie has never mentioned this dream to her teacher. The information the teacher receives from Jessie's dad, however, opens some new educational possibilities for the teacher and for Jessie.

Her teacher now can tailor Jessie's expanded curriculum to hook into her private passion. Without intruding on the student's obvious need for privacy regarding her future plans, the teacher can devise some "retail-related" activities. Jessie can use her math skills to practice inventory control or to figure out how to use marketing survey data. Her writing abilities can be practiced by creating a student-centered advertising campaign; she can use her analytical skills to compare successful and unsuccessful advertising campaigns. The teacher might invite a retailer to class one day to discuss the ups and downs of running one's own business.

The teacher also can be of great help to Jessie's dad. Although he knows about Jessie's fantasy, he may not know how to help her play with the idea of making it come true. The teacher might suggest that Jessie and her dad visit five toy stores and decide which ones are most child-friendly or which have the biggest selection or the most creative toys. Maybe the two of them can cook up a game or toy that would be available exclusively in Jessie's future store. The options are endless, and maybe someday Jessie will be a toy mogul. Or maybe not. Whether or not anything comes of it, Jessie will surely benefit from being taken seriously by her dad and spending time with him in activities that take her interests and skills into account. A teacher who is tuned into these interests can help make that happen.

"My school doesn't even have the basics!"

Many schools today have financial difficulties. When paper and textbooks are in short supply, there may be no gifted education specialists, special classes, or computers—none of the niceties found in schools with a full spectrum of resources.

Don't be totally discouraged. A broken-down building doesn't necessarily mean a broken-down education for your gifted child. The lack of a special program for gifted children doesn't have to mean a lack of hope. Some of the most exceptional teachers in the world are found in underserved, impoverished areas. Those teachers have chosen to be there, and by that very act have demonstrated a dedication to teaching that will serve your child well.

Even if the school is short on money, it has many human resources, and that's what a gifted student needs—human beings working together to create an active learning environment. If parents remain positive and demonstrate a strong commitment to their child's education, the teacher will sense that and respond. Wonderful things can happen even in the absence of money.

There are also national creative problem-solving programs that your school may participate in, such as *Future Problem Solving* and *Destination ImagiNation*, which provide challenging tasks for students to solve. There are many other state and national competitions that focus on academic achievement, such as *The National Spelling Bee, Knowledgemasters, The Geography Bee, Math Counts,* and *Science Olympiad.* Schools usually have information on these programs. Sometimes, it takes just one parent to request a program to get it started.

Some very needy schools have sent teams to these competitions. The school buildings may be old and need repair, but children, parents, and teachers are active and dedicated. Gifted children have great potential, and the parents and teachers have worked together to nurture that potential into full flowering. Where there is little money, there is simply a need for greater creativity.

Grants can help schools provide programming that would ordinarily not be available. "There's a lot of money out there to enhance school programs," says one school administrator, "but you have to look for it. Grant money is available from community foundations, the federal government, and other sources, for almost any kind of enrichment you'd like to see. You shouldn't try to write grants by yourself, though; you need the support of your district office. Parents and teachers should band together to see if school officials are paying enough attention to this type of activity. Writing grants takes many hours, but once you've done it a few times, you get to know the ropes and the funding sources. I wrote the first grant for our district; we received $25,000 a year for five years. We did amazing things with that money. If you want better things for your children and your students, you don't give up. You find a way to make it happen."

Chapter 6

The Classroom and Beyond: Learning Options for Gifted Children

A gifted program should not be a reward for good academics and high achievement. Remember, gifted students aren't always classroom stars. They become eligible for a gifted program not because of their current performance (although it may be exceptional), but because there are indicators (such as IQ scores, reasoning ability, outstanding reading or math skills, and the teacher's behavioral ratings) that these children need different and specialized educational experiences.

If one or more children in a regular classroom have been identified as gifted, there are a variety of ways to challenge and stimulate them with material and skills that match their current abilities and potential. Some of these strategies involve curricular acceleration—that is, speeding up the study of one or more subject areas. Other strategies involve approaches to enrich the child's curriculum or to provide for educational options through alternative structures.

Acceleration Options

Acceleration methods include *early entrance, curriculum compacting or telescoping, single subject (or focused) acceleration, whole grade acceleration (grade-skipping), concurrent enrollment,* and several other alternatives. Each has potential advantages, particularly for gifted children who are in the upper range of ability in one or more areas.

Early entrance is what it says: allowing a child entry into kindergarten, middle school, high school, or college before she has reached the traditional age for entry into these grades. Early entrance requires testing and agreement on the part of the school and the parents.

Early entrance into kindergarten is a big decision, but intellectually gifted children usually benefit from early admission.[18] Many gifted children need the challenge and despite the worries of some parents and teachers, they usually do well socially.

Curriculum compacting (or telescoping) is a type of acceleration that enables gifted students to skip work they have already mastered and move on to course material that more nearly matches their abilities, yet allows them to stay in the same classroom as their age peers. It lets students move through the grade level curriculum more quickly and avoids unnecessary repetition. Compacting requires that the teacher carefully conceptualize the learning objectives for a given subject, pre-test students for mastery of those objectives, allow students who pass the test to "telescope," and then design replacement or acceleration activities for these students. The activities might include alternative texts or supplemental material, small group or individual research, or self-directed units of study. Although the compacting process initially requires an investment of time from both students and teachers, it offers the potential for unleashing enormous creativity. Once the system is in place, it keeps gifted students from wasting their time, allows them to explore ideas and concepts in greater depth, and lets them practice higher level thinking skills as they solve more difficult problems.

---

[18]Rimm, S. B. (1994). *Keys to parenting the gifted child.* Hauppauge, NY: Barron's Educational Series, Inc.

Gifted children readily accept curriculum compacting once they realize that completing the basic curriculum means they have more time to do work that really interests them. As a result, they generally remain highly motivated.

Concurrent enrollment means that a child is enrolled in more than one program at the same time. For example, some gifted high school students may be enrolled in a neighborhood school and also in a different school that specializes in the student's area of interest. Elissa is such a student. She attends her regular high school in the morning and goes to a school for the performing arts every afternoon. Her classmate, Paulo, takes morning physics and calculus at a community college three days a week, but spends weekday afternoons at the high school where he takes his other classes.

Single subject (or focused) acceleration allows students the opportunity to move ahead one or more grade levels in an area of identified strength and has been heralded as a way to respond to both the intellectual and social needs of the child. He generally remains with age-mates for other subjects as music, art, and physical education and for lunch and recess. Since many young gifted children haven't yet developed their fine motor skills, they may also stay in their classroom for practice in handwriting or learning to create graphs. In the subject area in which the student is gifted, however, he is "accelerated" and meets with students of that grade level for that subject. For example, a second-grade student might go to the fourth grade for reading and the fifth grade for math, but stay in his own class for all other subjects and activities.

Whole grade acceleration, also called "skipping a grade," can be an effective means of helping gifted students achieve their potential, particularly those who are highly gifted. In a whole grade acceleration, a child is placed with his intellectual peers in the higher grades. Thus, from the time of the acceleration, the child spends her entire school career in the company of students who are not age-mates but are her academic equals.

Parents and educators often worry that the student's social and emotional needs may become a cause for concern. However, this often turns out to be less of an issue than might seem to be the case. Certainly, most middle school students don't want to pal around with a nine-year-old. However, if the child is thriving intellectually, parents often can find a way to get his social and emotional needs met through programs such as summer institutes for gifted students, sports teams, church choirs, Girl Scouts, Boy Scouts, or various volunteer programs. Research on students who have been grade-skipped shows that their social development has not been harmed. It might be more harmful to hold back their academic growth.

Some educators believe that skipping one grade is not enough, because curricular challenges don't change that much from one year to the next.[19] But a skip of two or more levels should be done only after careful consideration, particularly if it means accelerating an elementary school child to a middle school setting or a middle school student to the high school.

There are many aspects to consider when thinking about whole grade acceleration. The authors of the *Iowa Acceleration Scale*[20] have researched several factors related to school and academic performance: the grade placement under consideration; the current grade level of the child's siblings, because a variety of problems arise when a student is accelerated into a sibling's grade; the student's motivation and her attitude toward learning; the child's participation in school-sponsored extracurricular activities; and her academic self-concept. Developmental factors include age, physical size, and motor coordination. The child's interpersonal skills and the amount of support a whole grade acceleration will receive from parents and the school system must also be part of the decision-making process.

The *Iowa Acceleration Scale* contains a questionnaire to be filled out by a Child Study Team, which might include the school principal, school counselor and/or psychologist, the current classroom teacher, last year's classroom teacher, the gifted education teacher, the gifted education specialist, or any combination of professionals deemed appropriate. Based on the responses in the ques-

---

[19]Tolan, S. (1990). *Helping your highly gifted child*. ERIC EC Digest (E477). Reston, VA: The Council for Exceptional Children.
[20]Assouline, S., Colangelo, N., Lupkowski-Shoplik, A., & Lipscomb, J. (1988). *Iowa Acceleration Scale: A guide for whole-grade accerleration*. Scottsdale, AZ: Gifted Psychology Press.

tionnaire, this team can make decisions not only about whole grade acceleration, but also about other types of acceleration options that might be useful.

For example, Diana is intellectually able to handle a whole grade acceleration from middle school to ninth grade, but she has been elected captain of her middle school soccer team and believes they will be league champions the next school year. She is exceptionally close to her soccer teammates. A whole grade acceleration would mean leaving her school and her team. She, therefore, is highly opposed to the grade skip. Her parents also have major reservations. Based on these factors, the whole grade-skip option is ruled out; however, the group, using the information gained from the *Iowa Acceleration Scale* questionnaire, is able to come up with a recommendation. Diana will attend the high school for math only (single subject acceleration) and will pursue independent study in science at her middle school. She'll also continue playing soccer with her teammates.

Alternatives to Acceleration

There are methods besides acceleration that are also useful in providing the stimulation and challenge gifted students need to be engaged and excited in the classroom. These include, but are not limited to, cluster grouping, mentorships, gifted resource classes, and independent study.

Cluster grouping is used not only with gifted children, but also with children who are high achievers in a particular subject area. Students form small groups, or clusters, within their classroom and work together on a particular subject or content area such as math, reading, or scientific exploration. The clusters may be drawn from one classroom or might comprise students from a number of different classrooms. Wherever the students come from, they have similar needs and skills in a particular subject area. Cluster groups can be temporary and can be supervised by an experienced parent as well as by the teacher.

For example, a parent or teacher with special training in leading Junior Great Books™ discussion groups might come to school once a week to work with a multi-age cluster of gifted children who have been assigned to read one of the books in the series. There could be a similar temporary group that studies science topics with the help of parents who work in that field.

Cluster groups can also be permanent ones. A permanent cluster group includes all the gifted children from a single grade level. Here's how it works. Suppose an elementary school has 100 second-grade students, 25 in each of four classes. There are seven students who have been identified as gifted. But because the school has a limited budget, it has no gifted resource teacher and no special services for these students.

One way to serve these gifted children is to make sure that all of them are assigned to the same classroom and the same teacher. Research clearly demonstrates that gifted students need to be with other gifted children for at least part of every day. When they are grouped together, they enhance one another's learning, have more opportunities to form friendships, and are less likely to feel isolated. Such grouping increases the likelihood that their needs—academic as well as social and emotional—can be met through this permanent cluster.

Gifted resource (or "pull-out") classes contain only gifted students, typically meet once or twice per week, and are taught by a professional trained in gifted education. These classes provide opportunities for expansion of the curriculum, as well as the chance for gifted children to interact with other gifted students. Often the classes revolve around specific themes that are studied from many different angles, and there are frequently elaborate projects that involve the entire class. Students typically receive additional attention in areas such as research and reference procedures and in higher level, more complex thinking strategies.

In these pull-out classes, the special needs of gifted young students can be accommodated. Often a child who has been a problem for a classroom teacher finds his "place in the sun" in a gifted resource class and becomes much more calm when he returns to the regular classroom routine. Some parents report that their child enjoys school much more on the days he goes to the gifted resource room.

Some students who are silent in their regular classroom become talkative in the gifted resource room, sometimes overly so, because it is a place where they feel safe from ridicule and understood by both the teacher and the other students. One young student recently said, "Being in this class makes it possible for me to get through the rest of my week. It helps me so much to spend time with other kids who are like me."

As wonderful as these resource classes may be, they require a partnership between the resource and classroom teachers. Without such cooperation, students may be penalized by having to make up work they missed when they are not in their regular classroom. Also, the classroom teacher may not see the need for a gifted pull-out, believing that he can impart information just as successfully or that activities carried out in the gifted resource room should be available for every student. Unless the resource room activities are academically challenging, there may be criticism of this method.[21] Therefore, the pull-out program must be more than just enrichment activities that could benefit every student. For the resource room to be accepted by other teachers, work done there should involve higher-level thinking skills and greater academic rigor. The resource room must offer a differentiated program designed for the learning needs of gifted children.

Due to the movement of students in and out of today's classrooms, some teachers see pull-out classes as less disruptive than they might have seemed several years ago. Students go out for speech therapy or to be tutored in reading or for individual music instruction; others come into the classroom for mainstreaming in particular subjects. Gifted classes are just one more place a few students go for a class period every day or a half-day a week.

Pull-out classes, however, might bring another issue to the surface. Some high-achieving students (and their parents) want to know why they aren't included in the special program. "I'm smart," the students say. "My son tested in the 99th percentile in math and

---

[21]Cox, D. (1985). *Educating able learners.* Austin: University of Texas Press.

reading," the parents say. "Why isn't he in the gifted program?"

First, parents and children must be reassured that gifted programs aren't just about being "smart." There are smart, often very smart, students in every class. Gifted education is about "fit"—that is, providing students *who learn in a different way* with the curriculum that helps them learn best, just as schools provide a different curriculum for students who are slower learners. Smart children fit, and excel, in a regular classroom. It can be a disservice to a bright child who is excelling in regular classroom work to insist that the student be placed in a class for gifted learners, where she probably will not fare as well. Gifted students fit, and excel, in a class in which their opportunities for learning are deeper and broader than those of other students and where ideas and concepts are introduced far more rapidly. They require an *expanded curriculum* to meet their special needs.

Second, teachers can help parents understand the differences between ability and achievement. A high-achiever is not necessarily a gifted child, and a gifted child is not always a high achiever. *Achievement test* scores indicate what a child knows and can do. *Ability tests* assess reasoning and problem-solving abilities, as well as the ability to think in new and unusual ways. A bright child might, for example, test in the 98th percentile on an achievement test, but score far less on an ability test. That child is clearly very smart, but not gifted. A gifted child often will excel on both types of tests, but another equally gifted student might have surprisingly low scores on achievement tests. Gifted children sometimes do poorly on achievement tests because they may "tune out" during classroom drills and rote learning activities and therefore can't demonstrate what they've learned in the way the test asks them to. Or sometimes they overanalyze test questions and can't make decisions about true-false and multiple-choice test items. However, these students shine on ability tests, and their independent work shows originality and creativity.

The difference between the two types of testing can be confusing for parents and teachers. "There's no way Jason is gifted," says his teacher. "He doesn't do any work in my class, and he's failing in reading and geography."

But Jason is, in fact, gifted if his ability test scores fall within the gifted range, and he may be underachieving in class for a whole host of reasons. A gifted education specialist, trained to help gifted students, can intervene and assist Jason in discovering the things that motivate him to learn.

However, because the methods for identifying giftedness are not always perfect, there is always a possibility that a gifted student may have been overlooked and not included in the gifted program. Parents and teachers should then work together to see if a high-achieving student might qualify. Parents should collect evidence why they feel their child would particularly benefit from the program and talk with the teacher during a regular conference period or at a meeting they request. Maybe the child has written a television script based on a story the teacher taught in English class. Maybe he has gone far beyond the class in math by correctly completing the multiplication and division problems in an activity book at home. Parents can discuss their child's thirst for learning, which may not be evident to the teacher. Teachers should be open-minded about parents' observations and should refer the child for testing.

Some schools are willing to be somewhat flexible with their pull-out programs; they will serve talented students with the clear understanding that the students do not meet the strict entrance criteria for gifted identification. Other school districts require that students achieve a certain test score in order to attend a gifted program. Selection criteria is a local decision, but parents have a right to know what the criteria is. Sometimes decisions are settled by a Child Study Team that is committed to doing what's best for the child.

Mentorships provide an opportunity for the community to become involved with gifted education. A full mentorship usually occurs at the high school level, but some teachers use simple, short-term mentorships—or "shadowing"—with great success in both elementary and middle school.

There are many different ways to structure mentorship programs, but regardless, the value of a mentorship is enormous. For example, a high school mentorship program in one school district paired gifted students with adults in careers of interest to the student.

From this, the students gained an understanding of the realities of a future career and could make a more informed decision about whether they wished to pursue it. The students enrolled in this program participated in a post-graduate survey and reported that their mentorship was the single most valuable experience of their high school years.[22]

Lateesha participated in a career-oriented mentorship. Lateesha's father was a technologist at a local hospital, and Lateesha also had a gift for scientific inquiry. She decided to study the cleanliness of two waiting areas in the hospital: the general lobby and the emergency department waiting room.

With the permission of the hospital, Lateesha worked closely with a scientist in her father's laboratory, who taught her the scientific method and how to conduct field experiments. She then set out to do her research, taking cultures from several locations in both waiting areas. With the help of the scientist, Lateesha observed the progress of her cultures in the laboratory, identified what was growing in all those test tubes, and wrote up her findings in a report. She was surprised to discover both waiting areas were less contaminated than she had hypothesized. It was a fascinating study for her and her science class, and the hospital administration commended her for the work. They also saw to it that she got a write-up in the local paper.

Independent study allows students to work alone under the supervision of a teacher or mentor on special projects. It enables students to pursue areas of interest and offers opportunities for them to develop and use self-directed learning skills. Students who want to devote their attention to solving a real-world problem can be directed in designing original products and solutions. Often they can present their findings to appropriate audiences. Independent study should have some structure and be monitored by a teacher. At the high school level, it can be sometimes be structured to allow the student course credit.

---

[22]Reilly, J. (1992). *Mentorship: The essential guide for schools and business.* Scottsdale, AZ: Gifted Psychology Press.

Where Gifted Instruction Takes Place

These acceleration and other curriculum expansion methods can be provided to students in various ways. In some schools, the only option that exists is to provide services for gifted students in their own classrooms. Although generally this situation is not optimal, if the teacher can incorporate a variety of instructional accommodations, such as cluster grouping, compacting, learning contracts, independent study, original research, and mentorships for gifted students in the class, the regular classroom can be an exciting place for gifted students to learn.

Whether within a regular classroom or elsewhere, options can be structured in a variety of ways: a regular classroom with a differentiated curriculum and cluster grouping, self-contained gifted classes, a regular classroom with a pull-out class and cluster grouping, cross-grade classes with team teaching, honors classes, and advanced placement courses. At the other end of the spectrum are specialized programs: magnet schools organized around a particular discipline, such as fine arts or science, and rapidly accelerated programs for the highly gifted. The combinations are endless. A school district with a strong gifted program will have a variety of options for different types of gifted learners, rather than just having one kind of program.

The Guided Learning Plan

Gifted students often benefit from a Guided Learning Plan that sets out goals, objectives, and other parameters to ensure an optimal experience for the child. This plan makes it easier to implement and monitor the various specialized interventions the child needs.

Usually, a meeting of the Child Study Team is called to begin sketching out the plan. This school team develops a plan for any child with special educational needs and often consists of the counselor or school psychologist in addition to an administrator and one or more teachers. Most often, the team meets first to create a child's daily operational plan, and at a later meeting the plan and the rationale behind it are presented to the parents for their consideration and input. It's important to note that not every gifted child requires this kind of in-depth planning.

It's helpful for the child to have some voice in discussing any expanded or accelerated curriculum option. Gifted children are capable of participating in decision-making that affects their lives, and allowing them to do so helps enhance their tacit skills of self-direction and good judgment. Participation gives them a sense of control over at least a portion of their lives, and that sense of control goes a long way in preventing emotional and behavior problems. Obviously, adults will direct the process, but the child's viewpoint should be given as much consideration as possible.

Elements of a Guided Learning Plan

The Guided Learning Plan should describe:

- Behaviors or evidence that indicate that the child's needs are not being met by the standard curriculum.
- Strategies already implemented to allow the child to "opt out" of curriculum areas that have already been mastered. (Testing? Compacting? Single subject acceleration? Grade level acceleration? Independent study? Mentoring?)
- Additional methods, materials, experiences, or other services that might be chosen to more adequately meet the child's needs.
- Results that have already occurred, and results that can be expected as a consequence of implementing this plan.

A Sample Guided Learning Plan

Date_____

Student's name_____ Student's address _____

Gender_____ Birth Date _____

School_____

Current grade level_____ Grade point average (if applicable) _____

Child study team members: _____

_____

_____

Principal _____Current teacher _____

Parent(s) and or guardian(s)_____

Other (e.g., gifted education specialist, psychologist, counselor) _____

_____

Plan coordinator _____

Areas of Special Ability (Check all that apply and use comment section to indicate how the student has demonstrated exceptional ability):

☐ Math   Comments: _____

☐ Reading   Comments: _____

☐ Social Studies   Comments: _____

☐ Science   Comments: _____

☐ Art   Comments: _____

☐ Music   Comments: _____

☐ Other_____ Comments: _____

Ability Tests Completed:

Wechsler Intelligence Scale for Children (WISC-III)   Score_____ Date_____

Stanford-Binet Intelligence Scale (Binet 4)   Score_____ Date_____

Woodcock-Johnson Cognitive Ability Scale   Score_____ Date_____

Otis-Lennon School Ability Test   Score_____ Date_____

Cognitive Abilities Test   Score_____ Date_____

Slosson Intelligence Test   Score_____ Date_____

Other_____   Score_____ Date_____

A Sample Guided Learning Plan *(cont'd)*

Achievement Tests Completed:

Iowa Test of Basic Skills	Score_____	Date_____
California Achievement Test	Score_____	Date_____
Woodcock-Johnson Achievement Scale	Score_____	Date_____
Stanford Diagnostic Reading Test	Score_____	Date_____
Stanford Diagnostic Mathematics Test	Score_____	Date_____
Metropolitan Test of Readiness	Score_____	Date_____
Other_____	Score_____	Date_____

What other criteria are you using to verify that this student should be placed in a gifted program? _____

_____

_____

_____

_____

What adjustments have already been made to the student's current curriculum? (Check all that apply and use the comment section for additional clarification)

☐ Independent study   Comments: _____

☐ Cluster grouping   Comments: _____

☐ Mentorship   Comments: _____

☐ Early entry   Comments: _____

☐ Compacting   Comments: _____

☐ Subject matter acceleration   Comments: _____

☐ Whole grade acceleration   Comments: _____

☐ Prior inclusion in gifted program Comments: _____

Type of class_____

Date of placement_____

☐ Educational travel   Comments: _____

☐ Out-of-school classes   Comments: _____

A Sample Guided Learning Plan *(cont'd)*

Readiness:

On a scale of 1-10 (10 being the highest score):

Does the student attend school regularly and complete his or her assignments?	1 2 3 4 5 6 7 8 9 10
Does the student welcome academic challenge?	1 2 3 4 5 6 7 8 9 10
Does the student relate well to other students and to teachers?	1 2 3 4 5 6 7 8 9 10
Does the student behave appropriately, in and out of school?	1 2 3 4 5 6 7 8 9 10
Does the student participate in school life?	1 2 3 4 5 6 7 8 9 10
Is the student a leader?	1 2 3 4 5 6 7 8 9 10
Is the student enthusiastic about placement in a gifted program?	1 2 3 4 5 6 7 8 9 10
Do the student's parents want such a placement?	1 2 3 4 5 6 7 8 9 10

Expected outcomes and measurements to be used to monitor student's progress:

_____

_____

_____

Further recommendations for this student:

_____

_____

_____

_____

Teacher's notes, counselor's observations, or parents' comments can be added to this plan. The plan is then revisited yearly, or more often, if needed, to make sure the child is responding appropriately to the educational interventions and to make plans for the following year. It is signed by members of the Child Study Team and the parents.

Quick-Fix Solutions Don't Work

What's most important about the options for gifted students is that they be *ongoing*. It's easy to offer brief, patchwork activities and say that a gifted child's needs are being met. For example, ten-year-old Francesca goes to a gifted resource room every Thursday. That's good, but Francesca is gifted on Monday, Tuesday, Wednesday, and Friday, too, and she's equally gifted over the week-end, when she's totally beyond the teacher's supervision.

What the adults who care for Francesca need to do, then, is to confer, coordinate, and plan to make sure that her gifted experience is more than a break in a week of boredom and under-utilization of her abilities. Her classroom teacher needs to make sure she has extended curriculum or "beyond-the-umbrella" experiences every day. The regular classroom teacher needs significant communication both from Francesca's parents and from the gifted resource room teacher in order to give her what she needs on a continuous basis and to monitor her progress. It takes a little time and effort, but the results are worth it.

Is it Really a Gifted Curriculum?

Schools may advertise that they have a specific curriculum for gifted students, but on further investigation, it's not what is promised. Parents and community members will see most or all of these things in a good gifted program:

- An intellectual atmosphere where learning is valued
- Students who are actively involved and enthusiastic about learning
- Curriculum that meets students' developmental and academic readiness; differentiation of assignments to meet individual needs
- Independent learning and independent projects
- Problem-solving, open-ended tasks, and higher level thinking
- Creativity and divergent thinking (rather than a single right answer)
- Technology available to students for research and for daily work
- Comprehensive curriculum involving more than a single content area
- Students who are learning to understand and appreciate themselves and others
- Students who are exposed to areas for additional learning, such as career and college choice and possible future fields of study

In addition, parents will find that the school and the school district have:

- Teachers with training in the special needs of gifted students
- Administrators and faculty with knowledge of the special needs of gifted students and who are supportive of these needs
- A group of gifted students that contains approximately the same percent of different cultural and economic groups as the school or district as a whole
- A school board that supports the special needs of gifted students by providing funding for the program
- A school that is open and welcoming to parents of gifted children

Chapter 7

Making Choices: What's Best for Your Child?

Successful Solutions for Gifted Students

All of the instructional options mentioned in the last chapter represent a school or teacher's commitment to flexibility in gifted education. This kind of flexibility helps gifted children achieve their potential. But how will you know which methods work best for your child and when it's time for a change? The information below will give you some pointers.

Curriculum Compacting

What parents should know: Curriculum compacting allows students who have already mastered the skills and concepts of the regular curriculum to "test out" of that curriculum. They then use the time gained to pursue topics and activities that match their academic competence. For example, if Amy has already read the poems to be used in literature study and can show that she has mastered the required vocabulary and writing skills, she is then excused from reading the poems and filling out their accompanying worksheets. Instead, she is given an assignment to compare and contrast two works by the same poet or to write a report on how two poets treat the same subject. Her study has more depth and complexity than the work completed by the rest of the class.

To establish who is eligible for compacting, the teacher pretests all the children on the information they would be expected to know at the completion of the unit. Children who demonstrate proficiency on the pre-test are allowed to move ahead. Not every child who "tests out" of a particular unit is gifted, and sometimes a child will test well in one area and not in another.

Researchers at the University of Connecticut's National Research Center on the Gifted and Talented have discovered that compacting is possible in a wide range of classroom settings and can have positive results for both teachers and students. These researchers found that by pre-testing gifted students, teachers could eliminate approximately forty to fifty percent of the curriculum in one or more areas, including mathematics, science, language arts, and social studies, with no detrimental effects for the gifted children.[23]

Children for whom it's most appropriate: Compacting is important for the child who resists repetition *and* has proven he can work ahead without it. It's not beneficial for children who simply are impatient with drill. Students must demonstrate understanding of concepts before they may work their way through the material at a more rapid pace. Compacting is very attractive to a child who wants to do independent work. Demonstrating comprehension of the current curriculum can be the doorway through which the child must pass on the way to an independent project.

How to tell if it's working: When it's working, the student is able to stay on-task and to grasp more advanced concepts. If the child wanders away from the task or suddenly seems confused, he may be over-extended.

---

[23]Reis, S. M., et.al. (1993). *Why not let high ability students start school in January? The curriculum compacting study* (RM93106). Storrs, CT: The National Research Center on Gifted and Talented, University of Connecticut.

If it's not working: It's possible that the pre-test criteria were too non-specific, allowing children who weren't good candidates for compacting to enter into this curriculum modification option. In addition, some children, once they've tested out, get lazy and decide they don't want to make the effort necessary to gain the benefits of compacting. These children often begin to excel again if provided with a motivator, such as an incentive reward program. Ideally, children's motivation should be internally generated, but sometimes the parent or teacher needs to provide extra encouragement or incentives for awhile.

Finally, some students become temporarily anxious and overwhelmed if a large amount of new material is presented at one time; these same children calm down if the work is introduced in smaller chunks. If you see your child becoming nervous and edgy about the introduction of new content, talk things over with the teacher.

Cluster Grouping

What parents should know: As mentioned in Chapter 6, there are two types of cluster groups: 1) flexible groups based on interest and capability in particular subject areas and housed within the regular classroom, and 2) groups that cross grade levels and are formed to address the academic needs of students from many classrooms. Sometimes a cluster group is composed only of gifted students; sometimes it may include children who simply show an aptitude for a particular subject area and who will benefit from working with similarly talented students.

It's important to differentiate *high-ability* cluster groups from *mixed-ability* "cooperative learning" groups in which children work together on various types of learning projects. Although some research indicates that elementary school gifted students don't experience adverse effects from participating in such groups,[24] other teachers report that the gifted members of a

---

[24]Kenny, D. A., Archambault, F. X., Jr., & Hallmark, B. W. (1995). *The effects of group composition on gifted and non-gifted elementary students in cooperative learning groups* (RM 95116). Storrs, CT: The National Research Center on the Gifted and Talented, University of Connecticut.

mixed-ability cooperative learning group often take a larger share of the work, and that less able students are happy to let them do it. Gifted students may resent doing the majority of the work in such groups.

Cluster groups do not help gifted children if the groups are simply completing the same kinds of work that other students are doing. Instead, cluster groups must offer more and/or different opportunities; students must be challenged with activities and concepts that stretch their abilities. Cluster groups should offer gifted students a variety of enrichment and/or acceleration options.[25]

Children for whom it's most appropriate: Students who benefit from cluster groups are those who need greater depth and complexity of subject matter and are capable of being part of a small group. Not every student in a gifted cluster group needs to be gifted; some may be otherwise average students who perform exceptionally well in certain areas and benefit from a cluster placement.

How to tell if it's working: The group is purposeful and task-oriented; it self-corrects those who veer off-task.

If it's not working: Watch to see that the gifted child isn't stuck with the "leader" role in every group. The teacher must be wary about the gifted child's always being asked to be the leader while the others rest. Before work begins in a cluster, the teacher needs to spell out clearly that everyone has a part to play in the group. Assigning roles can help. One child, for example, could be given the task of recorder, taking notes and writing a report; another is assigned the task of gathering the books and other materials the group needs to do its work; and a third serves as overall project manager. Other students conduct research, design graphs and charts to illustrate the research findings, or do the actual class presentation.

If the students are off-task, fooling around, and not completing assignments, the teacher may change the criteria for inclusion or change the method of interaction with the group. He may need to provide more hands-on direction until the children develop the skills to work together effectively.

[25]Rogers, K. B. (1991). *The relationship of grouping practices on the education of the gifted and talented learner* (RBDM 9102). Storrs, CT: The National Research Center on the Gifted and Talented, University of Connecticut.

Independent Study

What parents should know: Independent study gives students an opportunity to study a special-interest topic in-depth and focuses on the child's specific needs and learning styles. If the child likes to work on defined projects, the study should be project-based; if the student loves math, math activities should be scattered liberally throughout the independent study. Independent study, although it provides freedom for the student, also needs to be carefully structured. Although the student may have intense interest in a subject, she may have little experience in some of the tasks related to data gathering, analysis, and presentation. The teacher provides instruction in these skills, outlines the steps of the study, and sets deadlines for the various stages of completion. Learning contracts between student and teacher are useful to keep independent studies on track. The results of the independent study are usually presented in some sort of forum to be evaluated by other students or by an outside expert.

Children for whom it's most appropriate: Independent study works well with children who are self-starters, require minimal guidance, are disciplined enough to work alone, and have the initiative and resourcefulness to do the necessary research. Because independent study requires a certain level of maturity, it is usually more beneficial for older students.

How to tell if it's working: The student stays on-task, maintains focus, and initiates ideas and projects. She seems absorbed in her purpose and the joy of discovery.

If it's not working: The teacher will have to provide more attention and structure to the independent study project. More frequent check-in periods with the teacher during which the child receives additional guidance will probably be necessary. If the light bulb of discovery continues to fade, however, a small cluster group may be a good substitute for independent work.

Single Subject (or Focused) Acceleration

What parents should know: Single subject acceleration is a useful tactic for the child whose achievement tests and daily performance indicate that he is at least one grade level ahead of age-mates in a particular subject area. The student may leave his classroom at a specific time each day to go to a higher grade for instruction in this subject area.

Perhaps the area of focused acceleration is math. It is essential that the child *not* be required to complete math work that he has already mastered. For example, a child who's taking fifth-grade math in the fourth grade should not be required to participate in fourth-grade math lessons in his regular classroom. That time should be used to practice new skills or to catch up on other work missed while the child was in the fifth-grade math classroom.

Teachers and parents considering single subject acceleration should be aware that they're setting up a chain of events that will last for years. If a child in the third grade is taking fourth-grade math, he will be doing fifth-grade math in the fourth grade, sixth-grade math in the fifth, and so on. As the child gets older, the acceleration classroom may be in another building, and transportation may need to be arranged. For the acceleration plan to be successful, parents, teachers, and children must all be committed to it and willing to do what's necessary to accommodate the child's learning on a continuing basis.

Children for whom it's most appropriate: This type of acceleration is best for the child who is capable of advanced level work in a particular area. Although the student's level of social competence—that is, the ability of the child to leave his home classroom to work with older students on the subject in which he excels—should be considered, it is a minor factor as long as the parents and school are supportive of the acceleration.

How to tell if it's working: The student feels challenged but not overwhelmed and looks forward to the academic time in the other classroom.

If it's not working: If the student fears leaving the classroom and is hesitant about joining the older group, help him locate a special friend who can serve as a mentor-guide to bridge the gap between the home classroom and the focused acceleration room. If the child is still uncomfortable and unhappy, the acceleration might have to be abandoned; the teacher will then need to incorporate accelerated content within the student's daily classroom activities.

Whole Grade Acceleration (Grade-Skipping)

What parents should know: Grade level acceleration may work for a student whose test scores, school performance, and teacher evaluations indicate that she is exceptional in all or most areas and has reasonable social and emotional maturity.

Children for whom it's most appropriate: This option is for the child who soars far ahead of age-mates in virtually all subjects and is able to cope with the pressures of being the youngest member of a classroom.

It is not enough that parents and teachers believe this kind of acceleration would be beneficial; the child must want it, too. Discussions with the student and family are imperative, so all the people involved have a clear picture of what this option will mean in terms of the child's daily interactions with peers and older classmates and what responsibilities the parents will have to assume.

These discussions should also deal with the issue of "failure." A child who tries acceleration—either single subject or grade level—and finds it too difficult may believe that she has to tough it out so as not to be seen as a failure. Counseling children before they enter into acceleration can help them understand that they are attempting something difficult and that they are to be praised for the attempt, even if they later decide it's too much for them to handle.

How to tell if it's working: The child is comfortable with older students, is not unduly stressed, and is able to keep up with the work.

If it's not working: Rather than skip an entire year at once, a student might, for example, compact the entire second-grade curriculum into the first semester and the third-grade curriculum into the second semester, thus making friends in both classes and being suitably challenged. By the end of the year, the child will be ready for fourth grade, instead of the third grade, but the learning will have been paced to meet the student's social as well as her academic needs. This type of acceleration requires close cooperation among teachers, administrators, and parents.

If the child feels out of place, dislikes the more advanced placement, and begins to suffer emotionally and socially, other options such as independent study or a mentorship might provide the child with intellectual stimulation, yet allow her social interactions with same-age peers.

Gifted Resource (or Pull-Out) Classes

What parents should know: The gifted resource room is a place where identified gifted students are gathered together for a specified amount of time each week. The group concentrates on tasks that require the children to exercise higher-order thinking skills. There are abundant opportunities for brainstorming, problem solving, simulations, and a variety of real-world activities and experiences. A resource room is most effective when the curriculum is interdisciplinary and uses wide-ranging themes that match the students' varied interests and ability to think globally.

Children for whom it's most appropriate: Gifted students who have independent research and study skills and the ability to interconnect subjects around a general theme profit most from gifted resource classes. The gifted children in the resource room frequently work around a key idea or issue and develop an advanced final project or activity that often requires an audience and some parental involvement.

How to tell if it's working: Students are eager to come to class; they are excited by the exploratory nature of the lessons that begin each unit of study. They bring in their own resources. They stop by the room during unscheduled periods. They offer the teacher their own ideas, which further expands the original course of study.

If the child is happy in the resource class, parents hear about it because it's major dinner table conversation. Parents sometimes tell teachers, "It's all she talks about. It's a place where she feels accepted and really learns."

"Coming here makes it possible for me to discover new things that are interesting to me," students say. The gifted resource room often relieves their feelings of impatience with the standard curriculum and gives them a sense of belonging.

If it's not working: The gifted resource room is not a panacea. If the student resists leaving the regular classroom and isn't interested in working on projects or subject matter outside of the resource class time period, teacher and parents need to confer.

There may be resistance from other teachers about activities in the gifted resource class, because students in these classes may be involved in activities that are "outside the umbrella" and even outside the general curriculum. However, gifted children require this kind of accommodation. To keep them interested and motivated, their education plan must be related to their interests.

Another possible problem is that students who attend a resource room may lose interest in the activities of the regular classroom, because the subjects there are taught at a lower level and a slower pace. A resource room model works best when there is continual communication and "checking" between the gifted resource teacher and the classroom teacher to monitor the child's progress in both settings. Frequent communication among the classroom teacher, gifted resource teacher, and gifted education specialist is also important. Parental feedback is helpful as well.

Self-Contained Gifted Seminars or Classes

What parents should know: Some districts use the talents of their gifted teachers in places other than resource rooms. Instead of a weekly or bi-weekly class, there are regular daily classes in subjects such as reading and math. The gifted student attends one or both. The classes meet the needs of these children every day, not just once or twice a week. This model provides the greatest amount of service to gifted students, as they are grouped with other gifted children and taught by a gifted education specialist for a portion of every day.

Children for whom it's most appropriate: Students who demonstrate their mastery of classroom concepts and show that they are capable of accelerated work do well with this type of instruction.

How to tell if it's working: Once again, students are happy. They are on top of the work, enjoy their peers, and feel challenged, but not out of their depth.

If it's not working: The child reaches a point where the work becomes too difficult. The student may require more one-on-one time with the gifted resource teacher, some peer tutoring, focused acceleration, or other curricular modifications that more precisely meet his needs.

Mentorships

What parents should know: A mentorship allows a student the opportunity to work with an adult professional in an area of special interest or talent. The length of a mentorship will vary with the age of the students. Students should begin with a day of *shadowing*, or observing the adult, and then progress to a short-term relationship, which for high school students, could later be expanded into an internship for college class credit.

Children for whom it's most appropriate: Job shadowing and short-term mentorships are useful for middle school students, while longer mentorships are most beneficial to high school students who are carefully examining a potential career field. Mentorships can also be valuable for gifted teenagers who are underachieving because they cannot see the relevance or practicality of their schoolwork. For a mentorship to be useful, students must have the ability to function appropriately in adult work settings. They should be given some instruction in dress and workplace etiquette before being turned loose. For accountability and for grading and credits, students may be required to submit a résumé, have an interview, and keep a log documenting their work experiences and observations. The teacher confers with the students periodically to help them evaluate the experience and relate it to future career choices or college fields of study.

How to tell if it's working: Mentorships work well when both the student and mentor are at ease, the student asks and receives answers to questions, and he fulfills assignments completely and thoughtfully. A mentorship should not be a "go-fer" job; to be a real learning experience for the student, there must be some depth and substance to the placement.

If it's not working: If students have to be coaxed to complete assignments, or if they tell you they're not well-matched with their mentors, it might be time for a change, either to another mentor or to an independent study. But before any action is taken, parents and teachers should meet to try to determine how to make the experience more meaningful and challenging.

Reality Check

Realistically, it's very difficult for teachers to sort out all of these options in the face of huge classes, limited time, and state mandates. It's impossible for them to analyze the needs of 30 or more individual students on a daily basis. There are, however, not that many truly gifted students who will cross their paths in a year, and it's worthwhile to help these students expand their learning options to the fullest—and for a very selfish reason. If the gifted student is fulfilled and happy, the teacher is, too. Getting a gifted child into the groove means a much happier child and a more relaxed classroom. As the parent of such a child, you might choose to gently point out to the teacher the possible advantages of giving your child some individual attention.

Avoid saying, "If you'd just give Bert some individual attention, he'd behave better." Try saying instead, "We've noticed at home that if we ask Bert what he'd like to learn or do, he tells us, and we can negotiate an activity we're all happy with."

All good teachers adjust the basic curriculum to some extent. They know which students need extra practice and devise ways for them to get it. Teachers encourage shy children by grouping them with others; they give early-flowering children additional responsibilities. They provide learning centers, contests, hands-on experiences, field trips, and access to computers. Good teachers also permit students to move around the classroom and pursue individual activities because they've discovered that there's an enormous waste of learning time when capable students, gifted or not, have to wait at their desks, minds wandering, for others to catch on to the day's lesson. Allowing flexible options recaptures wasted time and engages children in meaningful learning.

A teacher working with gifted students just has to go a little further, opening the spectrum of curriculum possibilities a little wider and giving special attention to the social and emotional needs of children whose intellectual growth has sometimes out-paced their ability to deal with their feelings.

Obviously, there are a number of flexibility options that allow gifted students to follow their interests without a tremendous amount of additional work on the part of teachers or parents. What's important for parents to remember is that meeting the needs of a gifted child is important to her growth and happiness, and that different educational choices may be appropriate at different times in the child's life. The option that's best is always the one based on the child's emerging needs, which continue to change as she grows and develops.

For example, while cluster groups may work well in the elementary grades, gifted high school students will perhaps learn more from a mentorship or independent study simply because they have now developed greater readiness and maturity. Also, it is a rare high school teacher who is able to institute cluster grouping for the 150 or more students that she sees daily. When sorting out the options, it's especially necessary for parents and teachers to keep in touch, so both can be on the lookout for changes in the child's behavior that indicate whether the flexible extension activity is a good fit.

Who's Responsible? Parents' and Teachers' Roles

Teachers, at least those in the same building, must communicate with each other about these special needs students. If Billy's first-grade teacher is going to allow him to compact the math curriculum, the second-grade teacher will need to know, because it will have ramifications for how she handles Billy's math instruction next year. It's not fair to Billy or to his second-grade teacher for the first-grade teacher to conduct these activities in a vacuum. She must share the plans with those who will be affected by the decision later—and with the school administration.

As a rule, teachers don't make these curriculum expansion decisions on their own. A Child Study Team should monitor Billy's progress at least once a year to determine what placements should be carried out over time. Billy's parents are an integral part of the decision-making process as well. Regular and frequent communication between and among all members of the child's team is the key to seamless transitions between grades and levels.

It's not a failure to admit that a student isn't profiting from a particular flexible pacing method. The teacher may simply need to fine-tune it or try another tactic. No one method is right for every child; part of the art of teaching is to match the child to the combination of strategies that will be most productive at the time, taking into account the student's need and readiness. Parents should give the child's teacher the support she needs as different options are tried out and assessed.

It's a good idea for parents to keep their own records of the expansion options that have been used. If, for some reason, the school doesn't pass on the information to guidance counselors at the middle school and high school levels, the parent can then supply the necessary data. Parents' records are also useful if the family moves to another location and a new school. Because of the sheer volume of students that middle school and high school teachers deal with every day, they are unable to tackle that sort of record-keeping. At times, it may become the parents' responsibility to make sure that their children don't fall between the cracks and end up in classroom situations that are inappropriate.

That happened once to Jake as he moved through the program outlined in the box on the following pages. When he made the jump from elementary to middle school, his records were a part of many files from many elementary schools. But because his mother had intimate knowledge of Jake's long-term program, she was able to assist teachers and counselors and make it easier for the school to place Jake where he needed to be.

In school districts fortunate enough to have a gifted education specialist, long-term planning is more easily implemented because the specialist helps facilitate communication among teachers and parents, as well as between grades and schools. However, with the increased mobility of families and the lack of trained professionals in some schools, there will be times when parents, like Jake's mother, will need to be the primary advocates for their child's ongoing flexible plan.

Short-term gifted programs that are nothing more than quick-solve scenarios unrelated to the child's curriculum are not very effective. Choices for gifted children must be part of an overall way of thinking about their education—an ongoing long-range plan that provides optimal learning and flexibility over the entire course of their school experience.

Gifted children are a diverse group. A single acceleration strategy will not work for every student; to give these young people the best chance for success, gifted programs must offer a variety of curriculum expansion choices. Here are two case studies that show how a single district met the needs of two very different students:

A Gifted Child's Progression: Jake

K-2: The gifted specialist conferred frequently with Jake's parents and teachers to see that he was provided with appropriate expansion activities in his home classroom.

Grades 3-6: Because of Jake's exceptional test scores in math, he was single subject accelerated. In Grade 3, he was placed with the fifth grade for his math activities; in Grade 4, he did seventh-grade math. In Grade 5, he continued his single subject acceleration, taking eighth-grade math. He completed middle school mathematics during Grade 6. This flexible pacing required cooperation and communication among his classroom teachers, other elementary teachers, and the middle school math teachers. In Grade 6, he also studied SAT (Scholastic Aptitude Test) guides and took the math and verbal practice tests to determine his skill level in math.

Grades 4-8: Jake was assigned to a gifted resource room one full day per week. He attended this resource room class through Grade 8. The class with other gifted children exposed him to economics, lab experiments, and architecture, all of which expanded his unusual abilities in math. However, in this classroom, he also discovered drama and ancient civilizations and polished his presentation skills.

Grades 6-8: Jake twice scored second place and once scored first place in the state math contest for middle school students. (Not all children enjoy these competitions, but Jake loved taking part in them.)

Grades 9-12: Jake used all he had learned through his acceleration and gifted program. He took a full complement of AP (Advanced Placement) classes and also participated in drama, track, and student government. He received a perfect score on both sections of the SAT. He was accepted at several top colleges and opted to continue his studies with a scholarship at a major university, where he is now a junior.

A Gifted Child's Progression: Lucy

Grades 2-5: Lucy, who had an IQ of 160, was introverted and very shy around her peers. Her grooming was haphazard and her clothes disheveled because her mind was on other things. She excelled in every academic discipline, but she was quiet about her achievements. Because she was considered socially immature for her age and there was little school support for whole grade acceleration, she was accelerated by subject only, working two years beyond her peers in both math and reading. She completed several independent study projects and took part in some career activities. A very conscientious student, Lucy went far beyond what was required in the classroom. For example, if a teacher mentioned a book another student might be interested in, Lucy would also go to the library as soon as possible and read the book cover to cover. Because she incorrectly assumed that her teacher's casual comments were assignments, Lucy worked several hours every night on "assignments" that had never been given. She became exhausted from her self-imposed regimen of study; her parents and teacher had to help her understand that a remark about a book or exhibit was not a command that she study the book or go to the exhibit, and that suggestions made to other students didn't apply to her.

Grade 6-7: Still single subject accelerated, Lucy now had a social awakening. In the past, she had ignored her same-age peers; now she wanted to be like them in every way. She adopted the clothing style of the other girls, listened to their favorite rock bands by the hour, read the teen magazines, and tried desperately to fit in. The "fit," however, simply wasn't there. She was two years ahead of her peers in her schoolwork and miles ahead of them in her interests. Deep in her heart, she really didn't care about the fads and crushes of girls her own age. She was interested in music, but not in listening to rock bands. Lucy nose-dived into a clinical depression, for which her parents sought immediate professional help.

Grade 8: Lucy begged to be allowed early entrance to high school. "I can't go back to middle school," she cried. "I know everything they're going to teach me, and the kids are so immature. I know I can handle high school work. Please let me try."

Due to Lucy's insistence, her parents, teachers, and counselors reviewed her work, her test scores, and her family situation, and they decided to petition the school administration to allow early entrance to high school. Such accelerations were virtually unheard of in Lucy's school district, but faced with a group of people who believed in Lucy's abilities and Lucy herself, the principals and superintendent relented, agreeing to a "trial acceleration."

Grade 10: Lucy bloomed in the high school setting. She had much more freedom to select from a broader range of courses; she joined the band and was also accompanist for the school choir. As she moved ahead in her classes, she began to take Advanced Placement courses. In her senior year, she was concurrently enrolled in a major university near her home. She was awarded several large scholarships at her graduation and today studies music theory and composition at a university far from her home.

Chapter 8

Learning Contracts:
What They Are and What They Do

The Value of Contracts

If your child comes home from school and tells you he has entered into a contract with a teacher, don't panic. He hasn't agreed to indentured servitude or committed you to providing cookies for the next five hundred school bake sales. Classroom contracts are nothing more than agreements drawn up between the student and teacher (with occasional parent participation as well). Not just for gifted children, contracts are useful for all kinds of students—those who are having difficulty and need a step-by-step process to help them progress, those who need extra supervision from parents and teachers, and students who are mastering new study skills.

For gifted students, however, contracts are often used as a management tool for teacher and student; they state what must be accomplished and assessed before a child is permitted to participate in expansion activities. They may also list curriculum expansion options.

Contracts are valuable because they give gifted children some areas of independent work, yet provide a path to follow. When contracts are used as an expansion option, they work like this: The students discover what the requirements are for a particular unit of study, what optional activities are available, and what they must do to earn the privilege of exercising those options. If they choose to follow the contract, there's virtually no limit to the ways they can expand their personal curriculum, and the contract helps them take responsibility for the learning activities they want to do. An important by-product of contracting is that the student gets to learn and practice negotiation skills and is more likely to feel involved in the educational process.

Because a contract is signed by both teacher and student (and should be available for viewing by the parent), you'll never have to hear "but that's not what the teacher said" arguments. A contract gives gifted children a dose of real-world learning. They catch on quickly that, in real life, a contract that's signed is an agreement that can be enforced—by both teacher and parent.

For gifted children, contracts are especially helpful in setting limits. Because they are so eager and curious, gifted children often want to study everything at once. It's easy for them to fly off in all directions, beginning project after project, only to abandon the activities when something more fascinating pops up on their radar screen. A contract helps them focus on one area at a time, a skill that will be essential as they progress through school and into their career paths.

Contracts are equally valuable for parents. First, a contract cuts down on disagreements about how long the child should study each evening. When you see that your child is actively engaged in meaningful learning, you are less likely to feel you have to impose a strict minute-by-minute regimen of study. That's a great relief to a child who doesn't need the nightly repetition of concepts that an average student might require. It's also a relief to you because homework is no longer a battleground.

Parents sometimes become concerned if their child seems to be wandering into optional areas and straying too far from the standard curriculum. They worry about whether their child will be ready for standardized tests, because she isn't preparing for the tests the way the other children are. A contract gives parents assurance that their child has mastered basic requirements and is up to speed with the state-approved curriculum before she is allowed to dive into the optional curriculum expansion activities.

Optional learning is the norm for gifted children. Gifted students often come to class already knowing what other students are often still struggling to learn, and they need to exercise their knowledge and skills in meaningful ways. Day-to-day operations of the classroom must be adapted for their needs, just as they would be for other children with special learning requirements. Thus, extended learning or curricular options should be the norm for gifted children.

Finally, simple contracts are very helpful to regular classroom teachers. As they walk around the room, observing students working in cluster groups or on independent studies, they're able to see whether any student is off-task and then gently point out the terms of the student-teacher-parent contract. Also, if the teacher must be away from the classroom because of illness, surgery, family emergency, or professional development, a substitute teacher can easily monitor the contract. The gifted child's important learning opportunities remain in place even when the teacher isn't there.

When the child ventures into the community to do research or to take part in a mentorship, the contract is part of the student's relationship with other adults who will be standing in for the teacher. The contract is a wonderful vehicle for gauging the effectiveness of an expansion option when the student is outside the classroom setting.

Developing and Using Contracts

Contracts can be simple two- or three-column working documents that are based directly on the general classroom lesson plan. Teachers usually don't need to create elaborate new teaching strategies for gifted students; it's enough to expand the basic course of study. The contract becomes the child's individual lesson plan. Students can offer their own suggestions for additional options and negotiate with the teacher for their inclusion in the contract.

Contracts needn't involve a great deal of additional paper-work, either. Students themselves should handle the check-off process and schedule their own conferences to share their work products. The students also should be responsible for the contract's safekeeping. If they lose it, they'll have to repeat a great deal of work. The contract is a valuable real-world learning experience for the student and a helpful tool for the teacher.

Contracts for gifted students begin with an understanding of what's expected at the end of the contract period—the goals and objectives for the unit. Once gifted children have the big pic-ture, they know what direction they're required to take and what they need to be able to demonstrate at the end of a unit of study. With the basics well described, they are capable of very rapid progress.

For example, let's say the unit topic is immigration in the United States. Before students can begin to work independently or in small groups, they need some frames of reference. The unit, therefore, may begin with an informal discussion session, which can include questions such as:

- What is immigration?
- Who are some famous immigrants?
- Where did they come from?
- What contributions did they make after they arrived in the United States?
- How does an immigrant become a citizen?

As the teacher listens to students' answers, he begins to get some sense of what they know and what they don't. The teacher may discover that the entire class is clueless and needs a few introductory lessons that provide basic vocabulary and concepts.

Immediately following the introductory lessons, the teacher pre-tests the class. The test includes all of the items the students will master by the end of the unit. The majority of children in the class will not earn a proficiency score of 80 percent or higher;

some, however, will. It would be waste of time and brain power to ask these children to sit still and re-absorb what they already know! They should not be expected to wait for the rest of the class to catch up. Instead, they must immediately be challenged with material that will engage and excite them. It's time to get them on an independent study contract.

Because of curricular and state mandates, contracts cannot simply be way-out lists of "fun" projects that have no relationship to the curriculum. Contracts must include both requirements *and* options. Students know that they must complete and be assessed on requirements before they may add optional activities. Requirements for the immigration unit might look like this:

- Pass, with at least 80 percent proficiency, a test on American citizenship and the Constitution (to help prepare for state proficiency testing in citizenship).
- Create a family tree that contains information on the student's immigrant ancestors (to develop research skills and to involve the parents in the child's learning experience). If the student is adopted, be aware he may be sensitive about it and not know which family to research. If the student displays great discomfort, find another option or talk with the student about the issue. Sometimes a conference is helpful.
- Devise graphs on immigration statistics during various periods of American history (to employ math skills).
- Research an ancestor's country of origin (to use map and geography skills).
- Pretend to be an immigrant and keep a journal about the experience (to enhance language skills)

Once the student has completed and been assessed on an the agreed-upon portion of the requirements, she is free to add optional activities, which might include:

- Researching the issue of illegal immigration.
- Creating a timeline of the discoveries of famous scientists who were immigrants.
- Building a scale model of the Statue of Liberty.
- Learning several phrases of an ancestor's language.
- Learning a folk tune or dance from one ancestor's country of origin.

The contract requirements reflect a variety of skills. Some requirements and optional activities are math and science-oriented, some stress geography or history, some place importance on art or music, while some emphasize language.

Gifted children will usually gravitate toward the contract options that allow them to follow their own interests and exercise their special gifts. That's perfectly all right, because if they are following the contract, their curricular requirements are being met, and many of the products of their optional study will be exceptional.

Examples of contracts between students and teachers are described on the following pages.

Sample Contract 1

Using this contract, students record points as they complete the work. The contract is broken into two parts so it doesn't seem quite so overwhelming to the student. For younger students, a teacher may develop more parts with fewer activities per part to avoid overwhelming the child with what looks like a tremendous scholastic load.

Sample Contract 1

Student's Name: Jane Metcalf | **Completion Date:**

Grade: 5 | **Subject:**

Teacher's name: Ms. Lopez

Immigration to the United States

Part I

Possible Points	Requirements	Points Received	Options
	Research five family members and significant family events to place in the *Special People and Events* book.		
	Become familiar with the Citizenship Test. Take the test yourself. Record your score.		Write a poem as a dedication to an immigrant ancestor.
	Complete a family tree, including dates of birth and death of ancestors. Transfer dates to timeline graph.		Complete an arrival box that contains simulated copies of the documents an immigrant needs to enter the country.
	Conduct a taped interview of a family member.		
	Complete math computations on the Statue of Liberty math sheet.		Make a map of your ancestors' travels from their country of origin through their arrival in the United States to the place where they originally settled.
	Write a description of a fictitious immigrant.		

Sample Contract 1 *(cont'd)*

Part II

Possible Points	Requirements	Points Received	Options
	Make a sample passport.		Build a scale model of the Statue of Liberty.
	Study immigration patterns. Transfer immigration statistics to a bar graph.		Write an immigration video script.
	Keep a simulated immigrant's daily journal (seven days minimum).		Draw or paint your family's arrival at Ellis Island.
	Write a dedication to a family member (one page).		Make a diorama of a boat coming into Ellis Island. Include the Statue of Liberty.
	Research an ancestor's country of origin and write a one-page summary of what you learned.		Research the issue of illegal immigration into the United States in the past ten years.
	Participate in the immigration simulation special event; for this event, create a costume similar to that worn by an ancestor, "land" at Ellis Island, and go through the entry process immigrants must use.		Create a timeline of discoveries of famous scientists who were immigrants.
Point Totals Possible		**Point Totals Received**	

Signed: _____
    Teacher

Signed: _____
    Student

In this contract covering the 60–day immigration unit, students earn a specific number of points for each completed requirement. After they've accumulated 150 points, they may choose one optional activity. Additional points may be used to choose additional activities. Points can also be used to calculate grades, if the child's school system requires letter grades. The child signing the contract is responsible for scheduling conferences with the teacher to demonstrate his work product, and he is in charge of totaling the points that allow a selection to be chosen from the option column.

This type of contract is relatively straightforward to create and implement, and it has a limited shelf life. This particular contract is just an example; many teachers prefer a contract without points or other external motivators.

Contracts needn't be as complex as the example above. Here are two other independent contracts that also work well.

Sample Contract 2

Name: Janette Reisner

Grade: 3

Date: January 16

Teacher: Mr. Santilli

Resource Teacher (if applicable): Ms. Paulson

Topic I want to study: Johnny Appleseed

I.   I will complete the following required activities:

    A.   I will receive at least an 85 on the unit test on the pioneers.

    B.   I will make a map of Johnny Appleseed's travels through the Midwest with a legend that shows how many miles he traveled.

    C.   I will complete an art project using apple seeds.

II.   I will need the following books to complete my study:

    A.   *John Chapman: The Man Who Was Johnny Appleseed* (Greene)

    B.   *Johnny Appleseed: God's Faithful Planter* (Collins)

    C.   *The Real Johnny Appleseed* (Lawlor)

III.   I will complete the following optional activities:

    A.   I will learn the names of the types of apples Johnny Appleseed planted and make a poster that tells the differences among them.

    B.   I will make an audiotape presentation about Johnny's relationship with the Native Americans he met in his travels.

    C.   I will prepare a timeline of events in American history that took place during the years of Johnny Appleseed's travels through the Midwest.

I will share my work by presenting a report with visuals. I will present my report by (Date _____).

I will have two conferences with Mr. Santilli on (dates) to make sure I am getting my work done in time to present my oral report.

Signed: Janette Reisner

Sample Contract 3

Name: Janette Reisner

Topic I want to study: Johnny Appleseed

I.   Here are the questions I plan to answer:

    A.   What are the myths about Johnny Appleseed? Why did these myths come about?

    B.   Where did Johnny Appleseed plant his orchards?

    C.   Do any of the orchards exist today? If not, are there any single trees that can be traced to him?

    D.   What major events in American history took place in his lifetime?

II. Here are the books and other materials I'll use:

    A.   The encyclopedia in the media center

    B.   *Folks Call Me Appleseed John* (Glass)

    C.   *Johnny Appleseed: A Poem* (Lindbergh)

    D.   *The Story of Johnny Appleseed* (Aliki)

    E.   The computer in the classroom

III. Here's how I'll share what I've learned:

    A.   Class presentation with two posters and a timeline.

Signed: Janette Reisner

Using contracts like these, students become responsible for some of their own learning, checking in with the teacher at agreed-upon intervals or if they require assistance. The contract promotes independence and motivation, and gives gifted students a sense of control and empowerment that greatly reduces the stress they may feel when they are forced into a step-by-step curriculum they've already surpassed. When stress is alleviated and gifted students are provided with the freedom and trust they deserve, parents and teachers will witness the gratifying development of these very capable children. These students are much more likely to become lifelong learners.

Section Three

Parenting and Teaching Strategies that Work

Chapter 9

Building Trust, Building Relationships

An Unexpected Emotion

When a child is first identified as gifted, parents usually feel a rush of excitement and pride. After the initial thrill wears off, however, they're likely to experience a surprising new emotion, one they're at a loss to understand. That emotion is fear.

Parents' fears are often expressed in questions such as:

- Am I smart enough to keep up with my child? What will happen if I'm not?
- Should I push my child or back off? If I don't push, will he become lazy? If I push too hard, will I harm him psychologically and make him angry and resentful?
- What if I don't have the time to give my child everything necessary to meet her needs? What if I can't find the money to provide the best education for her?

- Why are my child's moods so extreme? Is there something really wrong with her? What can I do to make things more pleasant?

Parents of gifted children are sometimes afraid to verbalize a fear that's common to almost all parents of special needs children—the fear that their child will be considered a "geek," a "nerd," unattractive, weird, or different—and will never be able to fit in or have any friends.

Perhaps the parents have always carried a mental picture of their son as being a class officer or a member of homecoming royalty. Now they're faced with a child who may have trouble getting along with age-mates, who finds school boring, who frequently challenges others' ideas, and who may be viewed by others as "too big for his britches." These aren't the behaviors that make children popular with peers and get them elected to leadership positions.

It can be a major adjustment for parents to reconcile dreams and expectations with reality. They may be confused or disappointed that their child is different from what they'd hoped for. They may be afraid to talk about their feelings with anyone, because society tells them that they "shouldn't feel that way" about their own children, particularly if they're lucky enough to have bright children.

It's essential, though, that parents confront and come to grips with their emotions. The sooner they stop trying to mold their children into society's or their own ideals and begin accepting them the way they are, the sooner they can become strong advocates for their children and help them develop their special gifts. It's really the use of those gifts—not just being class president—that will ultimately result in the child's being much happier and more fulfilled.

Being gifted doesn't mean your child won't do "regular kid" things. Lots of gifted children end up being class officers, cheerleaders, student government leaders, athletes, scholarship winners, and all sorts of things that make parents proud. In fact, when parents and teachers fully accept children as they are, they lift an enormous burden of stress from the children' shoulders. Such acceptance builds their self-esteem to the point that, even if they are different from other students, they understand that being different doesn't make them less than okay or somehow deficient.

It's paradoxical, but also true, that when gifted children are embraced for being who they are, they gain greater self-confidence, fit in better with classmates, participate in more extra-curricular activities, and are more likely to exercise leadership than if their parents and teachers are constantly trying to "help" them become more like their classmates.

Many gifted children have said that the people who have the greatest impact on their lives are those who:

- accept their feelings.
- love them, not just their gifts and talents.
- spend time with them.
- support their attempts, as well as their achievements.
- believe that learning is important.
- help them believe in themselves.
- encourage them to follow their dreams.
- give them focused attention.

This type of respect and regard is good for every child, but it's especially important for the growth and development of gifted children.

It might surprise you to know that when it comes to interacting with gifted children, teachers are fearful, too.
Teachers fear that:

- gifted students may know more than they do and will make them look ignorant in front of the rest of the class.
- gifted children will take all of their time and create hours of additional work.
- the children's parents will expect too much.
- they will not be able to challenge gifted children adequately.

While adults wrestle with these fears, gifted children are working on fears of their own. They're sometimes terrified because they believe that:

- they *are* weird and no one will ever like them.
- they must always have the right answer to every question.
- they may not be as smart as everyone thinks they are.

Because gifted children tend to have a more global perspective than their age-mates and are extremely sensitive as well, they are also sometimes very frightened about world issues such as war, famine, repression, torture, environmental pollution, crime, child abuse, and other serious problems. In addition, gifted children have vivid imaginations and carefully tuned antennae. Many of them anticipate an entire array of things that can go wrong in any situation. They rehearse and fret over every possibility, sometimes imagining actions and consequences far outside the realm of reality.

It's not unusual, then, for a gifted child to enter his classroom with considerable fear, to approach everyday activities with fear, and to embark on new relationships with fear. Because gifted children have such depth of emotion and are able to imagine or visualize many possible outcomes, relationships with others can seem very threatening. After all, though a relationship can provide joy, happiness, and fulfillment, it can also just as easily end in loss, ridicule, or misunderstanding—and they know it.

Therefore, the most important thing parents and teachers can do, long before they worry about cluster groups or mentoring, is to establish a trusting relationship with these gifted students. This gives the children safe havens, people to go to for help, and places where they can anchor themselves and rest.

The Most Important Factor

It's critical that gifted children be able to trust and rely on a minimum of two to three significant adults. They must know that these adults will act consistently and will always have their best interests at heart, even during periods of frustration and disagreement.

Children's peer relationships tend to ebb and flow. First there is one best friend, then another. Cliques form and disband, disagreements flare and are mended, trust is broken and reestablished. Most children can ride the wave, even if their feelings are hurt and their sensibilities bruised. But for gifted children, the risk is greater. Since the world is often unsympathetic to especially talented children, making friends with age peers can be very difficult. When gifted children do find other children who accept them, they may over-invest in the relationships. If the friends later betray that trust, the break feels irreparable to the gifted child, and the wound is slow to heal.

Parents and teachers, therefore, must be consistently trustworthy. Gifted children must be certain that the important adults in their lives will never ridicule them, put them down, or intentionally hurt them. These adults must be the ones whose regard for the child never falters, though interactions with them will at times be frustrating, perplexing, or exhausting.

One mother related, for example, that her daughter "had to cry every single night." Most adolescents are emotional, but every night? This mother was worried until she noticed that in the mornings, her child was cheerful, happy, and able to go about her life productively. Like many gifted children, she simply had an over-abundance of emotion that she needed to vent in the safety of her mother's presence. The mother stood by this child, night after night after night. Was she tired? You bet. Was she frustrated? Oh, yes. But was she also accepting and trustworthy? Completely—and this was an immense help to her intense, gifted, and sensitive child.

This kind of consistency in dealing with a child's feelings is hard to accomplish, and sometimes parents want to say, "Oh, come on! Janie didn't mean to hurt your feelings when she said she wanted to go to the movies just with Keshia; you'll go next time. Don't get so upset over nothing!" Parents must resist the temptation to criticize when the child is sharing feelings. If you want your child to continue to confide in you, you must validate those feelings, no matter how absurd they may seem to you. It doesn't mean you must agree that Janie is the meanest little child in the neighborhood. You know better. But you have to show that you understand how your child feels. It's the feelings about the facts, not the facts themselves, that matter to the child.

The Ten Commandments of Trust

There are several ways parents, teachers, and other adults can be the handholds in a gifted child's climb toward achievement and socialization. These following ten tips are helpful in rearing any child, but for gifted children, they are even more important, because gifted children's emotional characteristics and needs are often so much more intense than those of the average child.

1. *Give the child focused attention.*

Contrary to reports in the newspaper, quality time has little or nothing to do with trips to the zoo, the art museum, or the science center, although all of these activities can be worthwhile and entertaining.

Quality time, at least to a child, is having a parent or other significant adult's undivided attention, if only for a few minutes. To make your child feel important, you must really listen to him during that time. Eye contact is essential, for it's your eyes that tell the child you are totally focused on him for that moment.

Several years ago, a woman confided to a parent group that her talented husband was the most well-adjusted person she'd ever known. She then continued, "When I saw how his mother interacted with our children, it was as if a light bulb went on over my head. Whenever my children were talking with their grandmother, she sat with her chin in her hand, looking right at them and taking in every word they said. During those moments, they knew they were the most precious, important people in her life, because she was completely wrapped up in them. When I asked my husband about it, he said she had always listened to him that way, too. I'm sure his strong self-confidence today is largely due to her influence."

Parents' lives today are so busy that providing a child with focused attention on a regular basis may seem impossible. But it's not, because it doesn't have to be prolonged. A one-to-one or one-to-two "pow-wow" with Mom and/or Dad can occur over breakfast, before dinner preparations begin, the hour before bed, or the first few minutes after the child has actually crawled into bed.

If your child needs more attention than this, however, you have to be prepared to give it. No matter how crowded your life, your children must be your priority. There may be times in your child's life when he becomes excessively needy or emotional, and it feels as if he is draining you dry. You need to be there for the child during these periods. These times won't last forever, and once your child is reassured that your focused attention is available, his craving for it may diminish.

When you must cut a conversation short because of time demands or because something else needs your attention, try to remember where you left off. In all probability, the child will expect to pick up the topic again, and it shows real interest if you can say, "You know, we didn't finish our conversation the last time we were together. Have you thought any more about it?"

In the classroom, focused attention by the teacher can consist simply of brief teacher-student conferences a few times a week. It's not the teacher's job to be the parent, but parents do have the right to expect that their child will receive at least some degree of individual attention from the teacher.

2. *Provide ways for the child to communicate when you can't be there.*

In a home with one or two working parents and three children, a parent cannot be available for each child every single moment. Give the child who needs to communicate with you options to substitute for face-to-face meetings.

For example, give the child a cassette tape recorder or a note-book in which to write down things she would like to discuss with you later. This lowers the child's stress level, helps her get back on track, and makes it possible for you to give the necessary focused attention at a time when it's possible for you to do so. If you work, make sure your child checks in with you promptly and regularly after school.

If your child attends an after-school program, perhaps she can spend a few minutes jotting down the events of the day—and her feelings about those events—for conversation later in the evening. Sticky notes are valuable for on-the-run communication. When a parent or teacher is not available, students can write their questions and ideas on such notes, date them, and attach them to a bulletin board at home or at school, and the parent or teacher can get back to the child at the end of the day. The adults must be committed to dis-cussing the child's issues within a time frame that satisfies the child.

3. *Make sure your body language matches your words.*

Gifted children come equipped with their own set of truth sensors. Although most children can pick up incongruities between speech and body language, gifted children are exceptionally skilled at it, and when they observe a mismatch, they'll often call you on it. Or they may simply observe the incongruity, chalk you up as a hypocrite, and shut down altogether.

If you say you're not angry, but you're shouting or gritting your teeth, or if you're telling the child how interested you are in what's being said, but you're glancing at your watch every few seconds, be prepared to have the child notice and even point out the inconsistency in the message you're sending. This sometimes makes things worse, because now you may find yourself embar-rassed as well as angry or rushed. In such situations, it's best to be honest and say, "Yes, I'm angry because I asked you to move your science project out of the living room and it's still there," or "What you want to tell me is very important, but I have to leave for work in five minutes. Can you explain what you need quickly, or can we reserve some time tonight to talk about it?"

4. *Respect the child's privacy.*

Respecting privacy can be extremely difficult, particularly for parents who sometimes view a child as an extension of themselves, and especially if a child you love seems troubled. You may want to read that secret journal or go through a desk drawer. Resist the temptation. How would you feel if you found your best friend rummaging through your belongings or reading your diary? Believe me, the gifted child will feel the same way, only more so.

Once you've shattered a gifted child's trust, it could take months or even years to piece it back together, if it can be salvaged at all. Find other, more direct ways to try to discover what's going on. Ask the child point-blank what he is thinking or upset about. If you're the parent, seek out the teacher, and vice versa. Talk to a guidance counselor or other professional, but don't violate the child's belief in you by tearing down the wall of privacy or trampling on the boundaries to which everyone is entitled.

There is one exception to the privacy rule. If parents suspect that a child is engaged in something illegal or dangerous, they may have to resort to doing some detective work to prevent the child from coming to harm. It's best to get your suspicions out in the open, but if the child seems to be covering up a potentially dangerous situation, you may have to take measures you would otherwise avoid.

5. *Insist that the child respect your limits as well.*

Trust is a two-way street. You must earn it, and so must the child.

A few years ago, a father of a gifted teen came to a teacher and said, "My son is bigger now than I am physically, and he and I are butting heads about the telephone, of all things. His hormones are raging, and he's calling girls at all hours of the day and night. I'm afraid we're going to be arguing about this for months!"

"Take the phone out of his room," the teacher advised. "If he's making calls you don't approve of, take that privilege away until your trust is restored. It's not enough that he trusts you; he has to understand that you need to trust him, too."

The world in which gifted children will make their way has limits, and young people need to learn about those limits early in life. Gifted children are so curious and their energy levels are so high that they can spin out of control rapidly, trampling all over other people's rights and feelings. Reasonable limits and constraints, consistently applied, are often reassuring to a child who's going a million miles an hour and doesn't recognize that he is on the edge of "losing it."

Russell was such a child—charismatic, extremely handsome, athletic, and a true leader—but he was also manipulative, argumentative, and easily depressed if he wasn't in charge of his environment and the people in it. He could really stir up a class, and most of his teachers found him to be a difficult child. In his gifted resource class, he came into contact with students who were as intelligent as he. When he tried to manipulate and dominate them, it didn't work. There were frequent disagreements with other students. His teacher explained, "When I saw Russell becoming frustrated and ready to explode in anger, I would simply say, 'Russell, I think you're off the track a little bit. Before you and Amir continue your work together, maybe you'd like to do a little more research.' Then I'd lead him to the computer or give him some additional materials to study until he could calm down. Our communication system is so refined now that all I have to do is look at him in a certain way and he knows to back off and get himself together. It's interesting to me that he comes to see me the first thing every morning, just to blow off a little steam and get ready for the day. My room seems to be a safe place for him."

6. *Be prepared to explain rules and limits.*

Gifted children want answers. Why do I have to do my homework before I write in my journal? Why do I have to go to bed when I'd rather read for another hour? Why do I have to sit at the dinner table until everyone's finished eating? Why, why, why? All children ask these kinds of questions, but not all of them are capable of understanding the rationale behind rules and limits. Gifted children, however, can usually understand explanations, and they'll often accept limits once they see the reasons for them.

Evan, for example, was a gifted child who attended a resource class once a week. Somehow he got hold of a list of all the types of curricular extensions that were available at his school. A driven, competitive student, Evan approached his gifted resource teacher and asked him to intercede with his other teachers so that he could participate in every single one of them! He wanted to be in a math cluster, do an independent study, and be part of a mentorship program!

His teacher responded, "Evan, remember when you began coming to this class? You seemed comfortable with the blend of activities here and in your regular classroom. Have you changed your mind?"

"No," he replied, "but I want to go farther and do more. I love this class and I'd love school even more if I could do all of these things." Like many gifted children, Evan overestimated what he could take on and underestimated the time involved.

As the teacher related later, "It became a chess game. It wouldn't have been a good strategy for Evan to engage in everything he wanted to do. But he had a counter-argument for every point I made. Finally, I said, 'Evan, let's make a weekly schedule of everything you do now. I want you to put in all of your school activities as well as all your sports and church and family activities. Then we'll figure out how you'll handle the additional work these new extensions will require.' "

Evan made the chart, and although it was very full, he still believed he could shift activities and make the time necessary to take on the extra responsibilities.

His teacher, who knew how intense Evan was, finally said, "Let's look at one more thing. I want you to color-code this chart. Use red to color everything you think will cause you stress and make you tense. Color activities that give you pleasure in blue." When Evan returned the chart, it was virtually all red. His teacher spoke with him about the necessity for balance in one's life, and when Evan could visualize what the teacher was talking about, he stopped pushing for more work.

"I honestly believe that expanding his options any further would have taken him over the edge. He already put so much pressure on himself that he would have cracked under the strain of adding more work—and then trying to do it perfectly, which is the way he tried to do everything."

But be ready for some lively debate when it comes to setting limits. These children can think up more objections than a squadron of lawyers, and "because I said so" usually doesn't work with them. Adam, a gifted second-grader, had been taught since infancy to stop rudeness or out-of-control behavior by the time his parents counted to three. If his behavior didn't improve right away, he would face a consequence—usually a restriction of time that he could play a favorite game, watch a particular cartoon he enjoyed, or work on the computer. Recently, as his mother was counting, he stopped her and said, "What happens if I let you get to three?" Although she found the question very funny, Adam's mom kept a straight face as she told him what the consequence of his continued rude behavior would be. He looked at her for a long moment and said, "Okay, I guess I'd better stop."

Parents and teachers should also be prepared for some interesting attempts at manipulation. One mother related that she restricted her child's extracurricular activities until he began to complete his everyday schoolwork. Then, he suddenly started to fix her breakfast every morning! She, of course, wanted to melt into a little puddle, but fortunately, she saw through his plan to manipulate her and had the strength to resist it. She stuck to her position, and the schoolwork improved.

Although the question "Why?" may seem to be simply nettlesome, a gifted child's questions about limits can help you discover whether you're being needlessly restrictive. It's most effective to set rules about things that really matter, such as safety concerns or respect for others, and to adopt a more relaxed attitude about issues that aren't as important.

Remember, put in place only those rules and limits you can—and will—enforce. Idle threats are unproductive, and capable children see through them immediately.

The mother of a gifted preschooler reported that she had told her son that if he didn't pick up his toys, brush his teeth, and get into bed, he couldn't go to preschool the next day. He loved his school, and she thought this consequence would get his attention. "But then," she said, "it occurred to me that keeping him home was a punishment for me as well. I was scheduled to work that day, so preschool was as much a necessity for me as it was a pleasure for him. Now the consequence is the loss of *Sesame Street*. That affects only him."

Once you've set the limits that matter to you, however, enforce them consistently. Gifted children may test them more often than other children. You must respond consistently, even if you're as tired and cranky as the child. If she can get around you, the game's over.

7. *Respect the child's feelings, even if you must restrict behavior.*

A statement as simple as, "It's hard to wait, isn't it?" or "You're feeling hurt because Courtney teased you," validates the child's feelings. They need to be reassured that any feelings—even some that aren't so comfortable, such as anger or resentment—are okay, but that acting out those feelings by being rude, disrespectful, abusive, or unkind is most definitely not okay.

8. *Respect the child's confidences.*

Unless there are compelling reasons to break an agreement of confidentiality, things your children ask you to keep to yourself must not be shared. If, because of serious concerns, you feel you must breach the confidence, tell the child in advance and explain your reasons. Nothing will destroy trust faster than not honoring a child's confidences.

There are certain exceptions to this policy, however, and they involve confidences having to do with another's safety or health, such as hearing that your child's friend plans to take a weapon to school or that a friend who has been dealing with a substance abuse problem is using again. Your child may be upset that you have violated her confidence, but you can use the situation as a "teachable moment" regarding your ethical standards.

9. *Include the child in decisions that affect her life.*

Whether it's a decision about a curriculum expansion, a TV policy, or even a disciplinary issue, you won't get the child's cooperation unless she has been part of the decision-making process.

Gifted children often have very definite ideas about what's fair, unfair, rational, irrational, useful, or not useful, and they're capable both of stating their beliefs cogently and listening to yours intelligently. Bring the child on board; ask, "What do you think would be fair?" Listen to her answer, and you may arrive at inventive compromises together.

Katrina's mother gained her daughter's cooperation in establishing consequences for misbehavior. In a role reversal, the mother said, "Pretend you're the mother now, the adult. I'm the child. I've just broken a serious family rule. As my mother, what punishment do you think you should impose on me?"

Like many gifted children, Katrina held herself to very high standards; she came up with a more severe restriction than her mother would have asked for—and then accepted it willingly, because she'd been involved in deciding what disciplinary action should be taken.

10. *Tell the truth.*

If Grandma's sick or you're leaving your job, talk with the child about it honestly. Of course, you should consider the child's age and level of sophistication. The child, no matter how seemingly mature, is still a child and doesn't need to know every detail of Grandma's operation or that you're changing jobs because the boss is harassing you and other members of the staff.

Telling the truth, however, does not mean that you should make your gifted child your confidante in delicate family matters. For example, if parents are going through a divorce, they should remember that even though their child seems unusually mature and able to handle the situation, it is neither wise nor fair to share adult information or to expect the child to act as a peer. Adults with problems need to find other adults in whom to confide; they should spare the child the emotional turmoil of having to play the adult support role.

Within acceptable limits, though, be honest with your child. Gifted children have such fertile imaginations that the scenarios they picture in their minds can be much more alarming than the facts. Perhaps Grandma's operation was just to remove her gall bladder. If the surgery has been spoken of only in whispers, however, the child could come to believe that Grandma has a terminal illness and has gone to the hospital to die.

If you don't know the answer to a child's question, say so. Don't try to fake it. Gifted children can ask real stumpers. There's no shame in not having an immediate response. You can say, "I don't know. Let's go look it up," or "I'll try to find that out for you." Honesty is a key component in a trusting relationship. If you are honest, you will have the right to expect honesty from the child.

Flexibility and Autonomy

Establishing a safety zone of trust and honesty with your child will help banish the fear and nervousness that so often accompany the gifted child's intellectual package. But to help these children discover their true selves and their potential, you'll also need to give them wide latitude, autonomy, and lots of flexibility.

Some parents misunderstand the concept of flexibility. They think that to be flexible means to give a child free rein, to let him make demands on the family and essentially "run the show." Nothing could be further from the truth. All the flexing and extending and expanding that gifted children require should be carried out within carefully set limits, both at home and at school. Adults must always be in charge of the home and the classroom, because no matter how bright and capable the children appear, they don't really want to run the show. In their hearts, they know they aren't ready for that responsibility, so don't hand over your authority to a gifted child, even if he seems to be fighting for control.

But don't hold too tightly to old concepts about learning or discipline, either. In past generations, children often were disciplined with physical punishments, such as spanking; but in most homes today, that choice, though an option, is rarely made. Negotiation and the use of natural or logical consequences are the preferred methods of discipline today.[26] Similarly, just because you once sat in a classroom with twenty-four other children, never left your desk, heard lectures, and learned by rote and drill doesn't mean these approaches will work with a child today. Because gifted children have the ability to think analytically, they respond well to choices and options. They are able to understand reasons when adults take the time to explain.

Therefore, flexibility at home is as essential as it is in the classroom, unless you want to spend your time with a child who's frustrated, bored, anxious, depressed, combative, or withdrawn. A little give-and-take can make a real difference in a gifted child's quality of life.

---

[26]Dreikurs, R. & Soltz, V. (1992). *Children: The challenge.* New York: Plume.

Chapter 10

Accepting the Gifted Child

Have you ever heard any of the following from family members or teachers?

- "If he's so smart, why is he so disorganized? His homework is always late."
- "If she's gifted, why did she get two Cs on her report card?"
- "Giftedness is no excuse for interrupting others in the class."
- "Your son is deliberately trying to undermine my authority by asking questions he knows I can't answer."
- "Your daughter wants to talk all the time, and I have twenty-two other students to attend to. I can't spend all my time with her. If she's so gifted, she should be able to get it on her own, without help from me."
- "He may be smart, but his papers are a mess. I can't even read them."

- "Why do you allow him to question everything you say? You're the parent. Show some authority!"
- "He failed the test because it was multiple choice, and he wouldn't make any choices. He kept saying, 'It depends.'"

The people who make statements like this clearly don't understand how gifted children differ from other children and are therefore unable to accept their often complex and sometimes contradictory behavior. But acceptance is what gifted children, like all children, need most. They cannot thrive in an atmosphere that restricts them and stifles their intellectual, social, and emotional growth.

Developing an Accepting Attitude

How can people accept and warm to a child who challenges, interrupts, argues, and sometimes outshines them? They do it by realizing and remembering that *the child can't help being gifted*, any more than a hearing impaired child can help needing a hearing aid.

We can't condone bad behavior or make excuses for a child who is being obnoxious. As parents and teachers, part of our job is to help children learn skills that will make them acceptable to the rest of society. We have to recognize, however, that the gifted child's mind works differently from those of other children, just as the hearing impaired child's ears work differently.

Sometimes acceptance isn't easy, because the differences that characterize gifted children may show up in ways that aren't particularly attractive. Parents, teachers, and others who are involved with gifted children may have to endure arguing, over-emotionalism, intense questioning, disorganization, sloppiness, or interruptions. All of these types of behavior indicate asynchronous development—that is, a mind out of sync with the body. The mind is working at warp speed but residing in the body of a child—a child who has not yet developed either the maturity or the judgment to harness his impulses. How can we help such a child?

As parents or teachers, we wouldn't reject a child who was deaf. We would instead accept the child and work on whatever needed to be addressed to make him a functioning member of society. We must take the same approach with gifted children, accepting them as they are, nurturing their uniqueness, yet at the same time helping them modify behaviors that sometimes result in their being criticized or ostracized by their peers and by adults. Gifted children need our acceptance, help, and guidance. Expecting them to "shape up" on their own is like asking the deaf child to hear.

The Importance of Parents' Opinions

Parents are children's first mirrors. If what they see in those important mirrors is not unconditional love, joy, and acceptance, but instead disappointment, frustration, and anger, it can lead them to believe that they are not important or worthwhile. After all, if your parents, who are supposed to love you, can't accept you the way you are, what hope do you have that anyone else will ever like you? The importance of parents' acceptance of a child who may be different, difficult, and demanding cannot be overemphasized.

Are You an Accepting Parent?

Check to see how well you:

• *Listen to your child.*

Listening is the greatest gift you can give. Gifted children often need to work through their thoughts and ideas out loud, and a parent who is truly present during this process is a powerful source of self-esteem for the child.

The mother of a gifted kindergartner says, " I couldn't believe it! While I was fixing dinner, Tonia came into the kitchen and talked for a half hour, non-stop. All I said was, 'Oh, really? Why do you think that happened?' or 'How did you feel about that?' But you know, this one-sided conversation was really fun. Even though it was simply tons of words, she had a lot of interesting insights."

As adults, we know the power of listening. When we feel heard and understood, we also feel valued and validated. Children feel that way, too.

It's a fact, however, that "listening out" a gifted child can be exhausting, and sometimes you may need to call a halt. If that's necessary, be sensitive. You wouldn't tell your best friend, "Good grief, you've been talking for twenty minutes! Aren't you ever going to run down?" Don't say that to a child, either. Tell her how *you* feel, e.g., "Honey, I'm so interested in what you have to say, but my head is spinning with all the ideas you're talking about. I need a break. How about writing some of your thoughts down so we can discuss them later." In this way, you can avoid a blistering headache without hurting the child's feelings.

- *Support the child's interests.*

A parent offers this example: "I couldn't have cared less about the theater, but it was my daughter's passion. So I took her to plays and musicals every season." More than just taking her to performances, however, this father also found a way to enlist the stage manager at a local theater as a mentor for his daughter. The stage manager often took her backstage to meet the actors and occasionally made it possible for her to attend rehearsals. The father also found out all he could about children's theater opportunities in his area and arranged for his daughter to take a playwriting course and acting lessons with one of the companies. That's real parental acceptance.

Supporting a child's interests shows respect for his personhood, but don't kid yourself; it's not always easy. Dan's parents had always wanted him to be a doctor and were thrilled when he excelled in science and seemed interested in a medical career. His mother and father had big dreams for him: medical school, a fellowship at a major research center, and maybe the Nobel Prize.

When he was 16, however, Dan, who had always enjoyed cooking, suddenly announced that he wanted to become a chef. It was a huge blow to his family, and it was nearly impossible for them to shift their focus from medical school, stethoscopes, and MRIs to cooking school, pancake turners, and convection ovens. But they did their best, and strangely enough, after a long dalliance with food science, Dan decided he wanted to go to medical school after all.

Dan's parents were very wise. They could have insisted that he continue on the path they wanted him to follow and thereby set the stage for full-scale rebellion. Even after he'd changed his mind, Dan might have continued with his culinary career simply to thwart his parents and establish his independence. By accepting his wishes, his parents gave him the time and space he needed to experiment and then make his way back on his own. Dan became a doctor, but he's also a wonderful chef and uses his abilities in the kitchen to relieve the stresses of the day.

Because Dan's parents were accepting people, they would have supported him even if he had continued along his culinary path. They knew that their relationship with him—not his career choice—was what mattered most. They were not willing to sacrifice that relationship to win a power struggle about his vocation.

It's especially important for parents to realize that interests and careers are not sex-linked. Many gifted girls turn away from careers in math and science because society continues to tell them that these areas are just for men. Likewise, elementary school classrooms have lost some fine male teachers and hospitals have missed out on some talented nurses because elementary education and nursing are still sometimes perceived as woman's fields.

- *Praise your child appropriately.*

Praise is a tricky thing, because gifted children can see right through empty platitudes. They are very attuned to hypocrisy; they call it lying, and they're right.

In general, it's best to praise the effort, not the result, and to avoid such words as the *best, brilliant, magnificent, fantastic, the smartest,* and *unbelievable.*

Here's an example: Your child brings home a picture she's painted in art class. Do you say:

1. "That's just outstanding. You're the best artist in your class," or

2. "Wow! I can see you really worked hard on that. I like what you've done with the reds and blues here in the corner. What made you decide to use those colors together?"

The first comment may put tremendous pressure on the child for further excellence. She may feel she must now always be the best artist in the class or risk disappointing you.

The second response shows appreciation, not just for the product, but also for the work that went into it. It sends a strong positive message, and you've opened the door to further communication by asking a question about the artwork. If you were the child, which type of praise would you want? Praising the effort is also a useful strategy if the result of the project isn't very successful.

• *Avoid "put-downs."*

Words that are put-downs, such as l*azy, messy, inconsiderate, selfish, stupid, ugly, rude,* and *careless* clearly communicate non-acceptance, and they may also become self-fulfilling prophecies. When parents or teachers, who are children's most important authority figures, tell them they're lazy or sloppy, then in the children's minds, that becomes true. It should be no surprise, then, that the children may become lazier or sloppier than ever.

Correcting behavior is the flip side of praise, but the techniques are the same. Don't send *you-messages* such as, *"You're* driving me crazy," or "Why don't *you* ever do anything without an argument? Send *I-messages* such as, *"I* get so angry when I come downstairs in the morning and find dirty dishes all over the kitchen!" or " *I* felt so tired and impatient when we had that argument about taking out the trash." You've pinpointed the annoying behavior, and you've spared the child a damaging "put-down."

- *Respect the child's intelligence without being in awe of it.*

There will probably come a time when your child knows more about a subject than you do. Be happy about his knowledge, but don't be so impressed that you abandon your role as parent. The child hasn't grown up yet; he has overtaken you in only one small area of knowledge. No matter how much these children may know, they still need adult wisdom, maturity, and presence to feel "anchored"—safe, secure, and accepted. However, if the child has a passion for something you know nothing about, you can show your support and acceptance by enlisting a mentor who knows the subject.

Victor, for instance, was an enterprising and gifted student who had many interests that his parents just didn't understand. They were proud of his intellectual curiosity, and they had the money to provide things he needed for his investigations, but that was the extent of what they felt they could do. Because Victor was a self-starter, he put together his own group of mentors: one led him through the details of photography; one taught him Morse code and helped him earn his ham radio license; and one was an expert in the search for extra-terrestrial intelligence.

Not all children exhibit this much initiative, so you may have to be the one who looks for mentors for your child. It's in your own best interest to do so, because once the mentor is on the job, you have less of a burden of trying to keep up with all of the details of this aspect of your child's learning.

- *Help the child develop social skills.*

To be happy, children want and need friends. Gifted children are often intellectually far ahead of their age-mates yet may be socially far behind their intellectual peers. Thus, they may have difficulty finding buddies.

As a parent, you have experience in making friends, and you also have a child who probably displays some natural inclination toward ethical behavior and fair play. If you develop the child's inner compassion and ability to see the other person's point of view, you will go a long way toward helping your child achieve social success.

Hector's father was a psychologist who taught Hector about body language. After his father had spent considerable time instructing Hector about the meanings of various body postures and facial expressions, Hector became an expert in reading body language. For example, he could tell when other children were frightened, nervous, or confused simply by the way they stood or acted. This knowledge helped Hector become more understanding about other people's feelings. It heightened his natural empathy, and his insight made him well liked among his middle school peers.

Help your child learn to be modest and not brag about accomplishments, grades, or test scores. Without demeaning the child's achievements or comparing her favorably or unfavorably to others, point out the various types of talents that others possess. Intellectual ability is a wonderful attribute, of course, but so are artistic or musical talent, athletic ability, craftsmanship, and qualities such as persistence, kindness, helpfulness, and courtesy.

Gifted children are already set apart in so many ways; it's useful for them to understand that they are part of a larger whole, that there are many special people in the world, and that every human being is valuable. Do all you can to see that your child meets children and adults from other races, ethnicities, religions, and socioeconomic groups. It widens perspective and helps the child learn to respect all kinds of people.

- *Laugh with your child.*

Humor is a great tool for defusing tense situations or for just enjoying life. Some gifted children have a highly developed sense of humor, while others are stressed little people who need the emotional release provided by laughter and humor. Encourage your child to see the funny side of everyday life; share jokes and puns; laugh with pure delight at the witty things she says. Laughing releases endorphins in the brain and makes everyone feel better.

Are You an Accepting Teacher?

Teachers obviously have a powerful effect on children. How do you become the teacher that the gifted child will remember, not with despair, but with joy? Here's what some gifted students have said about teachers they liked and admired:

- "She trusted me with her video camera. I had to show her that I knew how to use it and take care of it, but once I did, she let me videotape the class presentations."
- "I wanted to study more complex systems, and he helped me do it."
- "She tells me why I'm supposed to learn certain things. Most teachers say, 'because it's on the test.' She takes the time to answer my questions and explain the reasons."
- "All my other teachers expect so much more of me. They think I should get A's on everything and never miss a question on a test. He's different. He's gotten to know me as a person, not just as a 'brain,' and that makes me want to try hard and do well in his class."
- "Some of my teachers have told me I'm too disorganized to succeed at anything. She said I was disorganized, too, but then she showed me some ways to manage my time and assignments better."
- "He treats me like the other kids, so I don't feel like some kind of weirdo."
- "She lets me try really hard stuff, and if I don't do well, she shows me where I made my mistakes, but she doesn't laugh at me and say I failed because I was trying to show off."

What are all these students really saying? They're telling us that their favorite teachers:

- empower them.
- encourage them to take risks.
- allow them to fail without calling them failures.
- respect them, both as unique individuals and as members of the class.

These teachers accept their gifted students, faults and all. Do you accept them too? Check to see if you:

- *Remain patient when gifted children ask questions, challenge your answers, or talk too much.*

If you grimace, frequently look exasperated, or sigh heavily when the gifted children in your classroom act like gifted children, you're sending a powerful message that they're somehow not okay, and by example, you're also letting all the other children in the class know that this particular group of children is not worthy of your acceptance. And if you don't accept them, why should the other students?

Remember that *these students can't help being gifted.* Because they think so fast, questioning, challenging, and talking too much are part of their general make-up. Of course, you can't allow these children to rule the classroom and trample all over the rights of other students. To keep that from happening, use teaching strategies that will both help them control their impulses and lead to optimal learning.

For example, if you're introducing a new literature study, ask your students in advance if any of them have read the book. You might find out that two of them, Reza and Hayley, have known the book backwards and forwards for the past two years. That's a valuable piece of information, because you can anticipate that these two students might be very disruptive to the group study. It's possible that they might blurt out the answers to questions, give away the ending, or laugh at others' attempts at understanding.

It will be advantageous to Hayley and Reza, as well as the rest of the class, to allow the two of them some alternatives in the literature project. Perhaps they can write about some aspect of the story in their journals; maybe they can work together to create alternative endings to the book or write short essays from one character's point of view. There are many ways to expand their learning while still keeping them part of the class.

- *Treat your gifted learners with the same respect you give other students.*

If not, you may be stigmatizing them. Parents have complained about teachers who sarcastically say, "Okay, all you gifted children, it's time for you to go to your special class." These same teachers would never say, "All you learning disabled children go to your special class now." Accept your gifted learners by letting them simply be members of the classroom and the school community.

- *Substitute meaningful lessons for rote learning.*

Do you agree that most gifted children don't need "more of the same" curriculum? Do you make specific plans to see that they don't have to participate in rote exercises that don't benefit them? If a gifted child has clearly demonstrated mastery of the concepts in a workbook, why should he complete three more exercises that review the concepts one more time?

Richard, age 7, has been counting money since he was four; he has always been the banker in family games such as Payday™. He can already handle simple fractions and is eager to learn division. Why, then, should he have to complete a series of lessons on counting coins? If his teacher insists that he "do what the others are doing," the most benign result will be that he's bored stiff. He may still need to study math computation, the same subject matter as his classmates, but he will also need alternative lessons that challenge his abilities and involve more complex transactions. Or he will need to be accelerated in math. Or have the curriculum compacted. Or use another alternative strategy that works for him.

Meaningful learning engages gifted children, and lack of challenge is one of the reasons gifted children are often late turning in their homework. The assignment is so easy it seems trivial, and who wants to waste time on trivial things? The gifted child figures she can dash it off at the last minute. But perhaps something intervenes: the child oversleeps, she gets interested in something else, or the bus arrives early. The "last minute" is gone, and the homework is late. More challenging homework can help this situation. As with daily classwork, gifted children don't need homework that simply reinforces already mastered subject matter; their homework should invite them to expand their current understanding. Yes, that may mean individualized assignments, but it will also mean that homework is turned in more frequently and the child learns more.

Some gifted children might like to negotiate with a teacher to design their own homework. Negotiation can be beneficial for both student and teacher; negotiation skills will serve the child well throughout his entire education, and negotiation can also build teacher-student relationships.

- *Understand that you may have to use different criteria to grade a gifted child's work.*

Gifted students often do poorly on true-false or multiple choice tests; they can have difficulty choosing only one answer because they can see how two, three, or even all of the answers might be true in differing circumstances. They may have trouble writing essays because of a tendency to overthink the question. They know the obvious answer, but often go far beyond what they've been asked. Their written response may have little relevance to the question because they've overshot the original idea. When it comes time to total up all the test grades, the final grade may be far lower than what the child deserves.

If you observe a big discrepancy between what you believe a student knows and the way he tests, it's possible that the error lies with the test rather than with the child. You might consider oral tests or some type of performance assessment to ascertain the child's true competency. Remember that most tests are set up so that average students can perform adequately. Adaptation of testing may be necessary for students who fall outside the average at both ends of the ability spectrum.

However, because proficiency tests are becoming the norm in many states, it's important that all students, including those who are gifted, be taught how to take these kinds of state achievement tests. States use the test scores to rate schools, so the stakes are high for teachers and school administrators. And once the students get to high school, the stakes are high for them as well. College entrance examinations are very similar in format to state proficiency examinations, so it's critical for students to learn the appropriate test-taking skills. Without specific instruction, some gifted children, who may have trouble with these types of tests, can freeze with anxiety on test day and do poorly.

- *Understand that a gifted child probably will not excel in every subject.*

Gifted children are usually better at some things than at others. Most of them have areas of specialization. They might be math prodigies or skilled verbally. Some are talented musicians or artists; others are science whizzes.

Don't expect outstanding performance in every aspect of academics. Gifted students, like others, can have deficiencies in a variety of skills. Many have terrible handwriting or can barely spell because their thinking speed so far outpaces their writing speed, or they've developed a personal shorthand to try to close the gap.

In math, they are sometimes unable to "show their work." Although they are often able to arrive at the correct answer by intuition, they seem unable to slow down enough to conceptualize the steps they took to solve the problem. Some students are incredibly disorganized, with desks that look like rats' nests. Gifted children who struggle with these issues need as much help as average students. Don't shortchange them. If they perform poorly in a scholastic area, don't put them down by saying, "You're supposed to be gifted." And don't excuse them from learning the strategies and skills that lead to success in the world as well as in the classroom.

- *Make time for discussion.*

Because of their incredible curiosity and their verbal ability, gifted children have an unusual need to ask questions and discuss issues in depth. "How can we learn if we never talk about anything?" they say. Discussion periods needn't be lengthy; a one-to-one conference when other children are involved in groups or completing individual assignments works well. The students can prepare for these student-teacher conferences by writing their questions in their journals or at the end of their homework assignments; this strategy gives the teacher a tool to keep the conversation on track and focused.

Acceptance and Advocacy: Cooperation for Results

The final stage of acceptance of your gifted child is advocacy—helping to develop the policies that govern the child's education. Both parents and teachers can be advocates at the classroom level, within the district, before the state legislature, or even in Washington, DC. One type of advocacy could be to form a support group for parents of gifted children within your school or district. A second would be to join a state association and attend its meetings and conferences to learn more about new theories, teaching strategies, and testing mandates, and to lobby for legislative activities in your state.

Gifted students with limited English proficiency, learning disabled students, minority children, and those with physical disabilities will often particularly need their parents and teachers to advocate for their inclusion in gifted programs. These children are under-represented in gifted instruction because of 1) *test bias*, for example, tests that favor English-speaking middle-class children; 2) *teacher bias*, that is, teachers who don't understand the ways that giftedness may be exhibited in minority students or in those with disabilities; and 3) *cultural bias*, that is, educators who don't understand how various cultural mandates can affect the way students perform.[27]

For example, a gifted Asian child working on a task may frequently ask for direction and guidance from the teacher because of the Asian cultural value of respect for the advice of those with greater experience. Other cultures, such as that of Native Americans, also emphasize the wisdom of elders and of those in authority.[28] Some cultures place greater stress on the attainments of the group, rather than on the achievements of one member. A native-born, middle class Caucasian child, however, probably has internalized the typically American values of independent thought and action. If teachers don't understand the cultural values of their ethnic students, they are likely to consider them less gifted.

As the child's parent, you, more than anyone else, know both your child and the culture he represents. You may have to persuade teachers and administrators to adopt a broader approach in assessing your child for a gifted program.

If you are not a native English speaker or you have a disability and need a translator, interpreter, or parent advocate to assist you on school visits, please notify the school in advance of your visit. You have a right to these services, but it sometimes takes a day or two to line them up. It's unfair to blame the school for not accommodating you if you've given them no chance to do so.

Although some parents will lobby on a state or national level, most parents will confine their advocacy efforts to the school system their child attends. If you find yourself in the role of advocate for your child or others in your school system, here are some important tips to remember.

- *Follow the chain of command.*

If you have an issue that's bothering you, go first to the child's teacher. Work with the teacher to try to make a change. If the two

---

[27]Frasier, M. M., Garcia, J. H., & Passow, A. H. (1995). *A review of assessment issues in gifted education and their implications for identifying gifted minority students* (RM95204). Storrs, CT: The National Research Center on the Gifted and Talented, University of Connecticut.

[28]Cohen, L. M. (1990). *Meeting the needs of gifted and talented language minority students.* ERIC Digest (E480). Reston, VA: ERIC Clearinghouse on Handicapped and Gifted Children.

of you can't solve the problem, ask the teacher to go with you to the principal. Issues can usually be resolved at this level. It should rarely be necessary to involve the superintendent or the school board, although there are cases in which this type of intervention becomes appropriate. If you go directly to the superintendent, you've ignored the chain of command and run the risk of alienating your child's teacher or principal.

A step-by-step approach to solving the problem may take a little longer, but if you want to change gifted education policies, it helps to have as many allies as possible. If you've ambushed a teacher or principal by going directly to their boss, they're far less likely to want to help you. It's much better to try to gain their support and goodwill so that they're willing to bolster your case if you need to take it higher up the ladder.

- *Advocate for all.*

Try to create change for every gifted student, not just for your son or daughter. You'll garner more attention and respect if you're working for an entire group of students, rather than expending all your efforts on your own family member.

- *Support the schools.*

Attend school board and parent-teacher organization meetings. Be visible and active. If there's a board election, levy campaign, or bond issue, work for passage and to get out the vote. Public school budgets are tight, and the very program you want for your child may be the one on the chopping block if a school funding campaign fails. Additionally, if you're in the trenches with the teachers and members of the administration during the tough times, they'll remember that when you make your case for gifted students.

- *Have a plan.*

Know what you want to accomplish, and keep your goals in mind. Listen to others' ideas and strategies. Remember that there are many routes to your destination. Be prepared to be flexible and to make compromises along the way. The end may justify a variety of means.

- *If you can avoid it, don't go to war.*

Simply making demands is a losing proposition. Resolve to work cooperatively with school officials to develop the best possible program. Engage, don't enrage. A little courtesy goes a long way. Behave maturely, and concentrate on issues, not emotions. Like everyone else, professional educators respond better to a reasoned presentation of evidence than they do to raw emotion.

- *Get the facts.*

Nothing undermines your position more than proceeding on the basis of half-truths and gossip. Get copies of existing policies; know and understand your state laws regarding gifted education. Keep current on research in the field. You may become a valuable source of information for school administrators who aren't up to date on every aspect of gifted education. Be sure to use your knowledge to help arrive at a team decision, not to publicly disparage the ideas of others.

- *Be persistent.*

Change is slow in institutions that are as large as school systems. You have to keep moving your agenda forward, inch by inch. Your faithfulness over the long haul may finally result in the changes you want, and your patience and fortitude will be powerful object lessons for your children.

- *Maintain a positive attitude.*

Remember that what you give out is what you get back. Negativity is catching. Most of those with whom you negotiate are people of good will, even though their opinions may differ from yours. Try to find areas where you agree and build on those.

- *Widen the circle.*

Enlist other like-minded parents, teachers, administrative personnel, and community members. Many brains are better than one when tackling complex issues. If your efforts and those of others don't work, you may need to try more formal approaches related to mediation or due process. Before doing so, however, be sure to look at the experiences of others that are described in three books by Frances A. Karnes and Ronald G. Marquardt: *Gifted Children and the Law: Mediation, Due Process and Court Cases; Gifted Children and Legal Issues: Parents' Stories of Hope;* and *Gifted Children and Legal Issues: An Update.*

- *When you get tired of it all (and you will), remember the children.*

If you are interested in becoming more active in advocating for gifted children at the state or national level—and many parents are tireless in their efforts to influence the creation and passage of laws that benefit this group of students—the National Association for Gifted Children has information, guides, publications, parenting information, public policy statements, legislative alerts, and more. The organization has affiliates in every state. Its Web site can be found at www.nagc.org. This will allow you to learn about what is happening in your state and nationally and to participate in the much-needed advocacy efforts.

Chapter 11

Supporting Gifted Children

All children need emotional and social support, but gifted children may need it more than most. Some gifted children feel isolated and peculiar. Many are perfectionists, with little tolerance for their own human errors. Some show signs of great stress. Some are excluded from their classmates' peer groups; they yearn for the friends and relationships other children take for granted, but lack the social skills to make friendships happen.

Although research shows that many gifted children have positive self-concepts, it's equally true that others have special needs related to their emotional health and social interactions.[29]

Some of the most common emotional issues gifted children face are:

- stress
- depression
- perfectionism
- friendships
- self-esteem

---

[29]Hoge, R. D. & Renzulli, J. S. (1991). *Self-Concept and the gifted child* (RBDM9104). Storrs, CT: The National Research Center on the Gifted and Talented, University of Connecticut.

Of course, many children are affected by these concerns, but gifted children can be affected to a greater degree—more stress, deeper depression, more intense perfectionism, lower self-esteem, and more painful loneliness. Parenting and teaching children who may seem to be bundles of raw nerves can be a tricky business. Where do we start?

Discipline and Limits: An Essential Supportive Strategy

One of the most important tasks of parents and teachers is discipline. Limits imposed by consistent discipline create the boundaries that give children a sense of predictability, a feeling that the world is a comprehensible place, and the opportunity to experience freedom within these limits. All children need limits and a sense of stability, but for gifted children, the feeling of safety and security that results from consistent discipline is particularly necessary. Gifted children have so many interests, so much energy, so much curiosity, so much emotion, so many ideas and concerns, and so much going on in their heads that they can rapidly feel overwhelmed, out of control, and frightened. The confusion engendered by fear and bewilderment can lead to a variety of emotional challenges. If rules, limits, and discipline are fair and consistent, it's sometimes possible to keep emotional upheavals to a minimum or even eliminate them altogether.

Children learn to discipline themselves by incorporating into their own self-concept the discipline applied to them by their parents and teachers. As they mature, they learn to apply this discipline to their own lives. Without self-discipline, children—gifted or not—will have a hard time achieving their potential. If they can't stay on track, finish what they start, and take responsibility for their actions, success will probably elude them.

Discipline and punishment are *not* the same thing. The words *discipline* and *disciple* have the same Latin root, a word that means *pupil* or *learner.* Disciplining children, then, means to make disciples of them—to help them learn the principles and values that we have found to be important for living a worthwhile, fulfilling life. The *only* way we can do that is to model those principles and values ourselves every day. As Bruno Bettelheim says in his book, *A Good Enough Parent,*[30] "We are all familiar with the old saying, 'Do as I say, not as I do,' but we are still loath to agree that this simply does not work when teaching children. Whether or not they obey our orders, deep down they are responding less to our commands than to their perception of our character and conduct."

If you don't model it, don't expect to see it. If you speak rudely to children, expect that they will learn to be rude to you and to others. If you scream and yell, be prepared for them to scream and yell as well. Conversely, if you treat children with respect, you will see them treat others respectfully. If you speak to them with courtesy, you'll generally get courteous responses. Consistent modeling helps bring about consistent behavior. Because of their intelligence and keen powers of observation, gifted children are quick to notice and take advantage of inconsistency.

Of course, there will be days when parents and teachers will be inconsistent, because adults are also subject to stress and worry. But if students are aware that their teachers and parents respect them, and if children are relatively sure of the consequences of their actions at home and in the classroom, their emotional lives become more stable. Adults who find themselves in unusually stressful circumstances, such as a divorce or job difficulties, are wise to seek outside help in handling their emotions. Bringing those stresses home or into the classroom can have a negative impact on young children.

The Power of Your Words

Rearing or teaching a gifted child can certainly try an adult's patience at times. But even when it's necessary to correct the child, the goal should be to encourage, not deflate, the child's enthusiasm, curiosity, and originality. Gifted children are often perfectionistic

[30]Bettelheim, B. (1998). *A good enough parent.* New York: Vintage.

and already hard on themselves; sometimes all it takes to change their behavior is to give them what parents sometimes call "the look." If more is required, however, adults need to find positive ways of pointing out what needs to be done. Gifted children are sensitive, and harsh words can break their spirits.

Interestingly, negative speech hurts the speaker as much as the listener. If parents and teachers are constantly putting a child or student down, using sarcasm, ridicule, and sweeping criticism, they will be feeding their own negativity—and negativity usually doesn't feel very good. Positive words encourage positive thoughts in both the speaker and the listener.

Negative and Deflating	Encouraging
J. J., why do I have to tell you everything 500 times?	J. J., I asked you to set the table 15 minutes ago. Please do it now so we can all have dinner.
Oh, goody, Mary Alice is going to share her great wisdom with us.	Mary Alice, I'm so happy you liked the story, but it's Serena's turn to speak now.
How do you expect to amount to anything if you won't do the simplest assignment?	Tell me why you don't want to do this assignment.
I am so ashamed of you! What gives you the right to be so rude to Ms. Donnolley?	You know we don't tolerate rudeness in our family, and today you were very rude to Ms. Donnolley. Can you think of any way to make things better?
Why don't you use the brains God gave you? You act like an idiot sometimes.	I was very disappointed in your judgment on the playground today. What are some other ways that you could handle a situation like that so you can avoid problems in the future?

Dealing with Life

It would be highly unusual for gifted children or any other children, for that matter, to sail through life without encountering hard times or making mistakes. They have to bump up against the reefs and rocks in order to learn and grow. Sometimes it's easy for them to right their own course. Sometimes they need help. Here are some potential problems to look out for.

Stress

Stress is part of everyday life, and all children need to deal with and manage their stresses. Children must learn to master challenges, meet goals and deadlines, and behave responsibly—and all of this learning is accompanied by a fair amount of stress. Certain types of stress can help children grow, find their life's purpose, and excel.

Sometimes, however, stress can overpower and distract them. Children generally don't have the strategies to deal with suffocating stress. Parents and teachers have to step in to teach and model the necessary coping skills.

What does stress look like?

In gifted children, stress can take many forms. Some children become so hyper that they are unable to concentrate or make decisions. Others become clingy, demanding constant support and reassurance. Some appear bored and unmotivated. Some develop school phobias.

Stress can also show itself physically. The children's posture may become tight and constricted, rather than relaxed. They may develop nervous habits or tics, such as biting their nails, stammering, or excessive eye-blinking. They may avoid eye contact and appear sullen and anti-social.

What are the reasons for stress?

Some reasons for stress are obvious: the death of a relative or cherished pet, break-up of the family, illness, relocation, a new sibling, or a newly blended family, to name a few.

Some stresses, however, arise from causes that are less clear-cut. They include:

- *Expectations that are too high.*

These expectations, which generally arise from myths about gifted children, may come from society, parents, teachers, or from the children themselves. Some adults believe, for example, that gifted children should receive A's in every subject, always "work up to their potential," do their best every day, always know the right answer, rise to the top in every activity, and always be mature and dependable. All of these unrealistic "shoulds" can add up to unbearable stress.

- *A concern for the world.*

Gifted children often have considerable global awareness. They may worry excessively about war, disease, starving children, earthquakes in faraway lands, violations of civil rights here and abroad, and the distribution of wealth. In addition, some gifted children believe that, because they have been given special talents, they must use them to solve the world's problems—right now. When they can't do so, they become frustrated and tense.

- *Overly intense parents.*

There's a fine line between encouraging children and pushing them. For example, a parent who notices that a child is verbally gifted and then requires the child to read aloud for an hour every day is pushing. That same parent could instead encourage the child's verbal gifts by giving her an endless source of story ideas through exposure to museums, neighborhood festivals, children's theater, and day trips. The parent could request a special story as a birthday or holiday gift. Forcing children to "use their gifts" in some structured, parent-imposed situation almost always results in considerable stress for the child.

- *Disconnected parents.*

On the other side of the continuum are parents who don't give the child enough structure or discipline. These parents take a hands-off approach, perhaps assuming that gifted children, who often seem like adults, don't require much parental involvement. Consequently, the children virtually rear themselves, and since they don't have the life management skills to parent themselves effectively, they are often highly stressed and confused.

* *Too many activities.*

Gifted children have so many interests that they may want to try everything from karate to student government to the science fair to hospital volunteering, and usually all at once. Although some gifted children can manage what appears to be a crushing load of academics and activities, others will become nervous and frustrated from spreading themselves too thin.

* *"Lack of fit."*[31]

In American schools, if a child is six, she is in first grade. For a six-year-old child who is able to master third- or fourth-grade work, however, the lack of fit between the child's capabilities and her placement in first grade can result in considerable stress.

This situation is like a school system's requiring that all children who weigh 40 pounds go to kindergarten; all those who weigh 50 pounds become first-graders, and all those who weigh 60 pounds are assigned to second grade. The majority of children will fit into the weight categories and be in the appropriate grade, but those who grow slowly might have to repeat a grade twice, while those who grow quickly might be pushed ahead too fast.

Age-related grade-level assignment works the same way. Children of average intelligence and social competence do well in their age-based grade-levels. Those who are a good bit smarter (or slower to learn) will suffer from lack of fit. Schools are designed to educate children who fit within the norm. Parents and teachers must advocate for those who fall above or below. To make the best assignments, schools must consider factors other than just age.

[31]Tolan, S. S. (1990). *Helping your highly gifted child.* ERIC Digest (E477). Reston, VA: ERIC Clearinghouse on Handicapped and Gifted Children.

• *Boredom.*

Not surprisingly, gifted children who are dealing with lack of fit are sometimes bored in school. Some experts theorize that nearly one-quarter to one-half of gifted children's time is spent waiting for the other students to catch up. That situation can be a recipe for disaster, because some gifted children who are bored may act out in the classroom. They aren't bad children; they're behaving badly because they lack the ability to cope with boredom. Having to do things they have already done many times creates stress that the children don't yet have the self-control or coping skills to manage.

However, adults need to be aware that some gifted children use boredom as an excuse to manipulate their way out of work they just don't feel like doing. In those cases, careful observation and communication between home and school can help the adults discern what's really going on.

• *Needless rigidity at home or in the classroom.*

A gifted adult recently told the following story: "I'm thirty-eight years old, but I remember it very clearly. I was in the fifth grade, and the teacher assigned us the task of writing a story called 'I Am the Clock on the Wall.'

"I thought about it and couldn't come up with much, so I used the clock as the jumping-off point for another story. I started with a boy looking at the clock, which somehow led him into daydreaming about traveling in space.

"I worked hard on my story. It was thirty pages long and really inventive. I described my space suit in detail, as well as what it felt like to be traveling in the cosmos. I wrote about the relationship of space and time.

"I got an F."

This man, who now excels in a highly creative profession, was the victim of an inflexible teacher who wanted a story *only* about a clock. The teacher refused to reward initiative and creativity, saving praise for only those who followed the assignment to the letter. Although it's possible the story wasn't worth an A, it certainly didn't deserve a failing grade.

Excessive rigidity and authoritarian discipline at home or at school can result in a power struggle. An overt power struggle occurs when a child, feeling unbearable pressure to measure up to unrealistic academic or behavioral standards, openly rebels, refusing to do homework or abide by family rules. Powerless to "get it right," he exerts what power he can by being defiant, and sometimes just plain nasty. Parents and child or teacher and child are locked in constant battle about virtually everything.

A power struggle can also take the form of underachievement. The child, knowing he can never get all A's, win every chess game, and be elected class president, simply gives up trying. Failing in school or at an activity a parent values serves two purposes for the child: it is a misguided way of taking charge of his own life, and it drives his parents to distraction. Young women who are subject to harsh, authoritarian parenting may decide that the only power they have is over their own bodies; they may become anorexic or bulimic in an attempt to maintain control. Gifted children are intense and strong-willed; when parent expectations become more important than the child's feelings, a long and bitter struggle may result.

- *Loneliness.*

It can be difficult for gifted children to find peers, particularly because their interests to do not fit with those of their age or classmates. Not many other first-grade children will be intensely interested in the classifications of dinosaurs and the era in which each lived, so a gifted child can have difficulty finding another child with whom to share his excitement. Other gifted children may be teased by classmates because they are so sensitive, intense, or curious, and may be called names like "nerd," "dork," or "baby." It's not surprising, then, that many gifted children feel out of place with their age-mates, and instead find refuge in books, or would rather spend more time with older children or adults.

What can you do to help?

• *Encourage the child to relax.*

Do grown-ups do their absolute best every single minute of the day? Or is their performance sometimes less than it could be? Why, then should adults demand perfection from a gifted student?

Gifted children oftentimes put a great deal of pressure on themselves to be excellent; they usually don't need anyone else adding more. In fact, one of the most helpful things parents and teachers can do is to lift the burden of impossible expectations by helping the child realize that he is human, will make mistakes, even fail, and that that's okay. Once again, praise the effort, not the result.

Remember that most children are gifted in one or two areas; don't expect them to stand out from the crowd in every subject.

And don't load them up with responsibilities. Young gifted children are intellectually advanced; that doesn't mean they have the practical knowledge to baby-sit siblings, prepare dinner, or take over the laundry. Teach them how to do these chores so they'll be ready to take them on when the time comes, but don't demand that they carry more than their share of family's work simply because they appear to be so capable.

Get involved with the child in activities outside the area of his giftedness. Take up sailing or bird-watching or cooking, and learn about this new activity together. Don't emphasize achievement in these activities; instead, focus on participation, fun, experimentation, and maybe even messiness. Activities in which the child is not expected to do better than everyone else are great stress-relievers.

In the classroom, be cautious about calling on the gifted child when all the others have tried and failed to answer a question. It's possible the gifted student doesn't know the answer either, or even if he does, perhaps he would rather not be singled out as the "class brain."

You can also teach the child specific stress reduction strategies, such as deep breathing, simple meditations, and progressive muscle relaxation.

- *Give the child outlets for his feelings of altruism.*

Although children cannot solve the problems of war and famine, there are actions they can take to help relieve suffering in their own communities.

One parent has been a cancer volunteer for years, taking food to cancer patients, driving them to doctors' appointments, and performing housekeeping duties. Her highly gifted young son has often accompanied her on these errands and has met many of the people she cares for. In his mother, he sees a living example of self-lessness. He has internalized this value, so it's no surprise that his friends seek him out when they have a problem. His compassion is quite remarkable for a nine-year-old.

Another parent has some homeless people on her social work caseload; she and her husband have taken their gifted seven-year-old son to family shelters, where he has seen first-hand what it means to be without the basic comforts of a home. He, too, is a compassionate child, and he and his parents often make selections of his toys to be given away to the children he's met at the shelter.

These children are learning that life can be hard and that human beings need to look out for one another. They have the self-satisfaction of being part of the solution, and it gives a special dimension to their lives.

Faith communities, charitable organizations, and scouting programs are good starting places for children to become involved. Of course, it's best if the parent is involved in these activities, too. Children learn best through example.

- *Do not over-emphasize conversation about scholastic achievement.*

Gifted children should not be given the idea that they're worthwhile only if they're making good grades, or that grades are the only things that matter. Instead, encourage them to take responsibility for their own learning by developing good study habits through setting aside a time and place for homework, by teaching them how to use resources such as dictionaries and encyclopedias, and perhaps by checking over their assignments.

Don't sit down with the child every night to "help" with homework. Don't constantly correct homework or make the child do it again and again until you think it's perfect. Don't finish an assignment the child "forgot" to do. If children are to develop the self-discipline to complete their homework adequately, they must face the repercussions of missing or incomplete assignments.

Natural consequences (that is, those that follow naturally from a particular action) are the best teachers. For example, if your child forgets his homework and calls from school, asking you to drop it off at school on your way to work, your first response might be to "rescue" him by doing what he asks. However, by not taking the homework to school, you allow him to experience the natural consequences of his forgetfulness. Once a child has suffered through natural consequences a few times, he probably will become more responsible without the need for the parents' intervention.

- *Monitor the child's activities.*

If a child is becoming overscheduled and stressed, sit down together and figure out which activities she values most and allow her to pursue one or two of those. Because gifted children can see so many possibilities and are often good at many things, making choices can be extremely difficult. Narrowing their options is often excruciating for them.

You can help by letting them know that cutting an activity out of their lives now doesn't mean that they can never pick it up again. Explain to them how rewarding it is to fully master an interest rather than to dabble in too many.

- *Help the child overcome lack of fit.*

The adults in the gifted child's life must work together to ensure that she receives the education that's most appropriate. There are still many myths about educating gifted children. Some of these myths include:

- *Gifted children must be kept with their age-mates.*
  Why? A child who is placed with intellectual peers

rather than age-mates for a significant portion of the school day will probably have fewer problems related to socialization than a child who's held back with children he can't relate to because they're too intellectually immature.

During the course of the child's school career, he will have many types of peers: sports peers, interest peers, and activity peers. Intellectual peers are just as important for the child, and it is unfair and counter-productive to deprive a child of intellectual peers in the very place dedicated to his education.

– *Gifted education is elitist.* If this is true, then the band is elitist, too, and so are sports teams and the debate club, because these groups are dedicated to the advancement of those who have shown special talent in those areas.

Why is special instruction for intellectual talent any more elitist than the special instruction provided for talented athletes? To encourage excellence, we must nurture the excellent, whether they are quarterbacks or physicists (or sometimes both at the same time).

– *Gifted classes put too much pressure on children.* Not true! Properly identified gifted children who are intellectually engaged and challenged are far less stressed than those who want to achieve but are thwarted by a lack of stimulation. Discrepancies between the child's ability and the opportunities provided by the school can be very stressful.

• *Emphasize what the child does well.*

Understand the child's way of looking at things and evaluate her work accordingly. If a child doesn't write exactly the story the teacher expected, draw precisely the picture that was assigned, or turn in homework that's identical to every other student's, the emphasis shouldn't be on what wasn't done, but on what was. Is the story inventive, the artwork outstanding, and the homework complete? Give a little. Teachers and parents cannot expect these children to act exactly like other children. Instead, they should help them find where they do "fit" and excel.

Depression

Unmitigated stress and excessive self-criticism can result in a gifted child's becoming depressed. Depression is more than just a case of the blues. It's a condition that must be taken seriously by both teachers and parents, because, left untreated, depression might lead to suicide. Not every depressed child becomes suicidal, but some gifted children do, and adults need to know what to watch for.

What does depression look like?

Like stress, depression has many signs. Be concerned if you see two or more of these signs: a loss of interest in activities that the child previously enjoyed, loss of friends, marked changes in eating habits and weight (either gain or loss), changes in sleep patterns (too much or too little), fidgeting, a drop in grades, restlessness or loss of energy, inability to concentrate, self-reproach, and thoughts of suicide. Young children may sometimes complain of frequent stomachaches or headaches; they may be irritable and look sad most of the time.

Any one of these symptoms, taken by itself, may be temporary or may simply be part of a child's make-up. Some children are naturally fidgety and restless; teenagers' sleep patterns may change; young children getting ready for a growth spurt may put on some weight; a heavy child may decide to go on a diet. Adolescents may retreat to their rooms more often; teens may also show less interest in family gatherings and outings. Although each of these things could cause worry among adults, one symptom from the list above doesn't necessarily signal depression. The presence of several symptoms, however, is cause for concern and possible evaluation by a psychologist or physician.

In most cases involving depression, the child has a pervading sense of sadness and feels that there is no way out of it. Many of the symptoms listed above are present. The child may say such things as, "I feel like I have a black cloud over my head all the time. It goes where I go." Or, "Who cares? Nobody." Or, "I'm so tired, and it feels like I'll never have any energy again." Or, "I wish I didn't have to wake up tomorrow."

Also, be aware that some gifted children are masters at hiding their depression. They may present a cheery facade and say all the right things. Others may mask their depression with anger, a "chip on the shoulder," or irritability that seems to say "keep away from me." Although most children will give clues to their state of mind, some won't. They can play-act so effectively that even their best friends, teachers, counselors, psychologists, and physicians don't suspect that the child is depressed. Many gifted children have an amazing ability to do and say the things they think adults expect and want from them.

Gifted children have the capacity to feel deeply and intensely. Sometimes their feelings are so painful that they try to shut them down altogether. The problem with shutting down feelings, however, is that the process is not selective. Although unpleasant feelings have been put to sleep, so have feelings of happiness, joy, and satisfaction. Depression sets in. Additionally, shutting down feelings is exhausting. The effort to "keep the lid on" can result in unbearable fatigue.

What are the reasons for depression?

In gifted children, depression often arises from *perfectionism*. Perfection may be impossible, but some gifted young people strive for it to their detriment.

A frustrated gifted boy once said, "I shouldn't have to go to school to learn. I should already know!" That's perfectionism squared. It's interesting to note that after a somewhat rocky adolescence, this young man grew up to be quite successful. He still expects too much of himself, but thrives in a high-pressure work environment in which he does many things very well, but not perfectly.

Depression can also be related to feelings of intense anger. In fact, one of the classic definitions of depression is "anger turned inward." That is, a child may be angry with friends, family members, or teachers, but rather than express the anger toward others, she turns it inward on herself. The result can be a severe depression.

Many gifted children go through at least one period of "existential depression."[32] This type of depression comes as a result of their working through the big questions of right and wrong, ethics and morals, the meaning of their own lives, and their mortality. After wrestling with these questions, they may come to believe that there are no right answers, no absolutes, and nothing to cling to, all of which makes them feel angry at life and then depressed. The depression may grow until they feel there's no purpose to life at all; things that used to matter become unimportant.

Other reasons for depression are related to those that cause stress: too much pressure to perform, too many activities, the inability to live up to others' expectations, feelings of isolation, and unreasonable guilt.

What can you do to help?

First, abandon the idea that depressed people are weak or that depression is a choice. Given the option, almost no one would choose to feel as sad and hopeless as depression makes one feel. Don't tell a depressed person, "Pull yourself up by your bootstraps." Would you tell someone in a full body cast to run a few laps around the track? No? Well, that's like telling a depressed child to stop feeling so sad.

Second, don't try to reason a depressed child out of her depression. Depression isn't reasonable, and reminding a child of

[32]Webb, J. T., Meckstroth, E. A., & Tolan, S. S. (1982). *Guiding the gifted child*, pp. 193-195.

all the reasons she *should* be happy can make her feel guilty, which may lead to even greater depression.

One helpful technique is *cognitive reappraisal.*[33] This involves teaching the child that feelings come about as a result of thoughts the child might not even be aware of. For example, let's say the child has received a failing grade on a test. The child's emotional response might be to feel worthless, but the thought behind the feeling could be, "I must never fail." If you can help the child examine the thoughts that result in negative feelings, you can sometimes help him develop healthier attitudes.

Child: "I'm worthless."

Adult: "Why do you think so?"

Child: "I failed the test and it was easy. I'm just stupid."

Adult: "Are you saying that only stupid people fail tests? Can you think of any other reason you might have done poorly? Was there something about this test that was difficult, even though you say the test was easy?"

Child: "Well, it should have been easy if I'm as smart as everyone says I am."

The child has now identified the crux of the problem. His failure on the test has made him feel terrible because he's trying to live up to an unrealistic standard. He has internalized a mistaken belief that being gifted means he must never make less than an "A."

Adult: "Do you believe that all gifted people do perfect work all the time? Can a person who's gifted ever make a mistake or fail?"

Child: "Well, we should do better than the other kids."

Adult: "Always?"

---

[33]Burns, D. (1999). *Feeling good: The new mood therapy.* New York: Avon.

Child:	"Most of the time."
Adult:	"And do you do better most of the time?"
Child:	"Yes, except on story problems."
Adult:	"Tell me about the test you failed."
Child:	"It had ten regular problems and ten story problems. I hate story problems."
Adult:	"Why?"
Child:	"I don't get them. I understand math problems I can see, but I get mixed up in story problems. It's hard to find out what the problem is all about. I'd rather do 'real' math. Story problems are just made up."

Now the child is really getting somewhere. He's moved from being globally "stupid" to stating that he has trouble with story problems. From this point on, the parent or teacher can suggest a variety of alternatives, such as peer tutoring or learning some specific tips for finding the "real math" in story problems.

Of course, this is an example on paper. Assisting an actual gifted child with a real issue won't be as simple as this, and a depressed child frequently has more than one concern. But it's comforting to realize that because gifted children are intellectually advanced, they can usually see the thought-feeling connection. Once they've discerned that the problem might be caused by the way they think about themselves rather than by something intrinsically wrong with them, they learn healthier coping methods, and the depression sometimes eases.

If a child of any age becomes depressed to the point that she can barely force herself to get out of bed, has constant insomnia, becomes anorexic or bulimic, tries to hurt herself, or talks about killing herself, parents should get professional help immediately. Call a suicide crisis line. If necessary, take the child to a hospital emergency department. Do not be embarrassed. Your child needs help, and you are the one who can see that she gets it.

Perfectionism

Perfectionism is the tendency to be unhappy with anything that isn't perfect or doesn't meet high standards. As Sylvia Rimm says in *Keys to Parenting the Gifted Child*, "Perfectionism goes beyond excellence: it leaves no room for error. The outcome must be the best."[34] Perfectionism is one of the most pervasive traits of gifted children, although it may be limited to only certain areas of the child's daily life. For instance, a child who is virtually obsessive about the perfection of school work may have a bedroom that resembles a dumpster.

What does perfectionism look like?

Perfectionism may show up in a variety of ways, some predictable, some surprising. Children who are unable to do perfect work often feel frustrated and angry. They may lash out at family and friends over little, insignificant things, or they may be very sad, even during fun activities. Sometimes, perfectionism is masked as underachievement. A child who has repeatedly failed to measure up to his self-imposed standards may simply stop trying. He may refuse to do homework or study for exams and in general become a classic underachiever.

What are the reasons for perfectionism?

Gifted children's perfectionism is related to their asynchronous development.[35] Remember Jenny, the little girl who wanted to write, but whose fine motor skills weren't developed yet? She's a typical example. A gifted five-year-old may have an eight- or ten- or even a twelve-year-old's picture in her mind's eye of what a painting, essay, or a relationship should look like. But when she can't measure up to her imagining, the child becomes distraught.

---

[34]Rimm, S. (1994). *Keys to parenting the gifted child.* Hauppauge, NY: Barron's Educational Series, Inc.

[35]Silverman, L. K. (1993). *A developmental model for counseling the gifted.* In L. K. Silverman (Ed.), *Counseling the gifted and talented*, pp. 57-59. Denver, CO: Love Publishing Company.

What can you do to help?

Having high expectations is not a bad thing in and of itself. Stand-outs in any profession are likely to have perfectionistic tendencies. From Thomas Jefferson to Albert Einstein to Sally Ride, people with high standards are found in every walk of life, and they make great contributions in their fields.

The adults in a gifted child's life need to help her realize that setting high standards is an admirable quality and that striving after excellence is a good thing. But they must also help the child understand that not meeting exceptionally high standards is not a reason for depression or loss of self-worth. Gifted children must know that the value of striving is in the act itself, not necessarily in the result.

In addition, adults should point out to these children that failures are great teachers. All innovators have learned from the hundreds, maybe even thousands, of mistakes behind them. Mistakes and discarded hypotheses are the scaffolding on which these people have built their success. It's sometimes as necessary to find out what doesn't work as it is to discover what does. It's helpful if parents and teachers point out mistakes they've made to gifted children and laugh about them. "Remember the time I left the baking powder out of that blueberry recipe? Wow, that cake was really flat. But we ate it all anyway. It wasn't perfect, but it was still good."

In addition, remind the child that she can't expect to do something perfectly the first time she tries it. How many times has an Olympic skier fallen before she became proficient enough to win the medal? How many times did Beethoven rewrite portions of the Fifth Symphony before it became a masterpiece? So how likely is it that a gifted child will learn cursive writing the first day? How many mistakes will it take before she masters all the intricacies of the scientific method?

Beyond helping the child develop realistic expectations, parents and teachers can suggest some daily strategies that might increase the odds of performing successfully. They include:

- *Maintaining good health habits.*

The chances of a child's meeting his goals are dramatically lowered if he doesn't get enough sleep, eat a healthful diet, and refrain from mind-altering substances.

- *Practicing time management.*

If a child wishes to achieve on a particular project or test, he must allow enough time to complete the project or study adequately for the test.

Gifted children learn very quickly, and they sometimes don't see the need for taking daily steps toward a goal. If there's going to be a unit test, for example, they may wait until the night before the test to read the entire unit. The cramming technique sometimes works, because these children can process a great deal of information in a short time, but it creates stress, and if it isn't effective, the result can be an embarrassing failure.

Parents and teachers can introduce children to time management techniques appropriate to their developmental stages. A six-year-old with limited small muscle control might not be receptive to keeping a written calendar, but he might be willing to use a computerized model that requires mouse clicks rather than writing.

- *Setting goals and priorities.*

In life, not everything people attempt will have perfect results. Adults generally place the greatest emphasis on matters of highest priority, and we can teach children to use that strategy too.

By talking with the child, we can help her discern what is most important to her and assist her in setting priorities and timelines for achieving her goal. When children realize that they need to conserve energy for areas of importance to them, they are less inclined to expend their efforts trying to achieve excellence across a broad spectrum of activities.

Many gifted children participate in too many extra-curricular activities, and this sort of priority-setting may help them discover which activities really matter and which they should drop.

Friendships

Because of their asynchronous development, it can be hard for gifted children to find day-to-day friends. This can be a source of frustration for them, and they may feel lonely. Their mentors may be considerably older and busy with their own lives, their age-mates may be too immature, and their intellectual peers may consider the younger gifted child an inappropriate or unsuitable friend.

What do friendship issues look like?

Finding friends is a big issue for gifted children. Sometimes the major friendship issue is that there don't seem to be any friends around. Conversely, if the child "makes the rounds," trying to find a group to fit into, there may be almost too many age-mates around, but few real friends.

What are the reasons for friendship issues?

There are several:

- When she latches on to a compatible friend, the gifted child may wear out the new acquaintance by demanding excessive emotional closeness and intimacy.
- The gifted child who is perfectionistic might demand the same high standards in her friends; most people won't measure up.
- Some children may not have the self-confidence to be a friend to a child who is much brighter than they are. They may view the gifted child as conceited and stuck up. Children who feel threatened by another's gifts can be very cruel—taunting, teasing, and bullying the gifted child.
- Younger gifted children can be bossy, telling other children how to do their work and insisting on enforc-

ing the rules in every game. Naturally, other children avoid "the bossy kid."

What can you do to help?

Gifted children have a strong need to know they aren't "nerds" or "weirdoes." The best way for them to find that out is to become acquainted with other gifted children.

Get involved in a support group for parents of gifted children[36] and help your child meet other gifted children. Investigate summer institutes or other types of intensive programs that bring gifted children together where they discover many others like them. In these experiences, isolation vanishes as the children work together on projects that interest and challenge them.

Friendships that grow during summer experiences don't have to end when the program ends. Summer friends may churn out e-mails several times a week, either continuing to work together on a specific interest or just to keep in touch. The sphere of friendship for a gifted child can be virtually unlimited, because such children can be found in every city in the world, and Internet and e-mail communication make even intercontinental relationships possible. Of course, it's a given that parents and teachers must advocate for ways to group gifted children together as often as possible during the school day or week. Even the most wonderful on-line friendship can't substitute for real-time friends at school. Special programs give gifted children a place to be together and feel accepted and valued.

Another way to help your child with friendships is to foster the gifted children's natural empathy and compassion. When gifted children learn that they must be respectful of everyone, not just persons of high ability, it helps transform bossiness into leadership and tones down the need for perfection in relationships.

The strongest models of compassion and friendship are always the child's parents. You can show your gifted child how to

---

[36]Webb, J. T. & Devries, A. (1998). *Gifted parent groups: The SENG model.* Scottsdale, AZ: Gifted Psychology Press. (SENG stands for Supporting Emotional Needs of Gifted).

be a friend, standing by your own friends in time of need, being happy for them when they succeed, and lending a listening ear. And most important, the best way to make sure a gifted child has a friend is to be that friend.

Self-Esteem

Many adults are puzzled that children who are so bright should have issues with self-esteem. Nevertheless, many of these children do. Many gifted children are as intensively evaluative of themselves as they are of others and are filled with self-doubt.

What does low self-esteem look like?

Low self-esteem doesn't exist by itself. It's a symptom of many of the other issues discussed above. For instance, a child who is constantly criticized by others is likely to have low self-esteem. A child struggling with perfectionism may experience a dip in self-esteem in the face of what he considers to be repeated failures. A stressed-out child may concurrently suffer from low self-esteem. A child who can't find friends will almost surely develop some loss of self-worth.

What can you do to help?

In an effort to build the child's self-esteem, parents and teachers sometimes fail to notice or address the underlying issues, such as perfectionism or stress. They concentrate instead on the symptom; they may attempt to deal with the child's poor self-image by leaning on a superficial self-esteem curriculum or by trying a variety of parenting methods believed to have positive effects on children's self-esteem. However, if the child's primary issues aren't dealt with, his self-esteem is likely to remain low.

Some self-esteem exercises for the classroom can actually have disastrous results if there are no back-up plans that ensure inclusion of every child. For example, a teacher in a suburban district explains how she had the children form a bridge, and as each child passed under, the others were to say nice things about him or her. For the majority of children, this was a positive experience, but when the class's only highly gifted child passed under the bridge, there was complete silence. The children weren't being intentionally cruel; they simply couldn't relate to this little girl. They didn't know what to say, so they didn't say anything. You can imagine the result.

In another classroom, middle-schoolers built mailboxes into which each student was to place letters to classmates, once again saying positive things or asking a question. However, the exercise hadn't been set up correctly, and the so-called popular crowd got stacks of mail, while one classmate received no messages. "I felt completely invisible," he says. "I couldn't figure out what it meant. Did my classmates dislike me or were they just indifferent to me, which in some ways is worse than getting hate mail."

Teachers who use self-esteem exercises in the classroom need to build in safety measures that guarantee no child will suffer or be left out. They must monitor such activities very carefully. One kindergarten teacher handled the self-esteem curriculum very creatively. Each child in her classroom was given a week as the "star" of the bulletin board. There was a large poster of the child, examples of his or her work, and positive quotes from other students in the class. When one of the students died of leukemia six years later, the family displayed the poster from that long-ago kindergarten class at the funeral home. It obviously had been an important moment in the student's tragically short life.

Authentic self-esteem results from being accepted for who you are. It comes from being valued, cared for, and understood. Self-esteem also comes from mastering challenges and using one's talents to the fullest. Parents are the primary source of unconditional love, acceptance, and appropriate discipline—all of which feed and nourish the child's self-esteem.

But teachers are also in a position to offer challenges to be mastered, opportunities for success, and positive reinforcement that allow the gifted child to grow intellectually and socially to reach full potential.

Books: A Powerful Ally

One way both parents and teachers can help gifted children cope with stress, depression, perfectionism, friendship issues, and low self-esteem is through *bibliotherapy*—the use of literature to help children understand and solve problems.[37] Bibliotherapy is one way gifted children can learn to recognize their emotions and deal with them. There are a variety of children's books and stories that reflect the issues gifted children sometimes face, such as loneliness, being "different," and family problems. Some are non-fiction books aimed specifically at gifted children, and some are novels or short stories that discuss the issues through narrative and dialogue.

Bibliotherapy allows children to feel safe while they explore the emotions that trouble them. When they identify with the characters in a story, they can examine and recognize their own concerns and puzzlements. They begin to interpret and apply the lessons of the literature to their own lives, "trying on" various ideas and solutions, first at a distance and then, perhaps, in their real lives. This technique can be used effectively with different ages and allows a way for children and adolescents to feel less alone by knowing that others have survived similar experiences.

Bibliotherapy is a two-person activity. It's not enough to hand a child a book and hope he sees himself in it. The child needs to discuss the book with an accepting adult who knows how to ask open-ended questions, listen carefully to the answers, and keep the conversation moving. That person could be a teacher, librarian, counselor, or parent.

---

[37]Halsted, J. W. (1994). *Some of my best friends are books*. Scottsdale, AZ: Gifted Psychology Press.

Chapter 12

Working Together for the Child's Sake

Cooperate Whenever You Can

Parents and teachers are a safety net in a gifted child's world—a world that may not understand the child's uniqueness. In an ideal situation, parents and teachers are allies in educating the student. It makes gifted children feel more secure to know that these important people are working side by side in their desire to do what's best for the children. But whether they get along or sometimes hold different opinions, parents and teachers should try to present a united front to the child.

When You Must Part Company: Your Child Comes First

Unfortunately, many situations involving gifted children's education are not ideal, and in those instances, your child's welfare must come before loyalty to a particular teacher, school, or school district. The more that teachers and administrators know about gifted children and the more training they have in working with them, the more likely they are to be supportive of the interventions a gifted child needs.[38] It's a fact, though, that the majority of teachers, psychologists, counselors, and other school personnel have had little exposure to or training about the needs of gifted students. This group of people is not particularly hostile to gifted students; they just don't know what to do with them. In schools and classrooms staffed by these untrained educators, gifted children may suffer from inattention and lack of stimulation.

There are a very few teachers who would be better off in another occupation—those who use humiliation and punishment to keep students in line, those whose classroom management styles include only regimentation and rote learning rather than discussion or exploration, and those who are cold and distant. These teachers can do serious damage to a gifted child's academic, social, and emotional life. If your gifted child tells you that he's unchallenged and bored in school, or worse, if he starts to share stories of verbal abuse, sarcasm, and unfair treatment, you need to check the situation out. But don't immediately jump to the conclusion that your child is 100 percent right and the teacher 100 percent wrong.

Even the most gifted child can make a mistake in judgment, and most children, gifted or not, occasionally moan and groan about their schools, teachers, and principals. Students may not like a teacher for a whole host of reasons: he's too "strict" (which may mean he manages his classroom well); or she's "weird" (which may mean that her hairstyle isn't up to date). If your child is voicing a series of run-of-the-mill complaints and can't give you substantive descriptions of specific incidents, it might be best to let him work through the difficulty with the teacher—with your help and guidance. You should ask for a conference with the teacher to make your own assessment of your child's concerns. If the teacher appears competent to you and his explanations are reasonable and satisfactory, there's probably no reason to make a change in your child's classroom

---

[38]Clark, B. *Growing up gifted*, p. 166.

assignment. This is a time for you to help your child learn how to interact successfully with people he may not like very well. It's a life lesson all children need, because in the real world they'll be required to work with all sorts of people they might not choose as friends.

However, if your conference with the teacher convinces you that she doesn't have the expertise to make modifications to the curriculum, doesn't believe in programming for gifted children, or shows evidence of being spiteful and punitive, you must take action to remove your child from this unfulfilling, potentially toxic environment. Check with other parents, too; the teacher could also be acting inappropriately with your child's classmates.

Older children's judgment about teachers is usually highly developed. Once again, a few isolated incidents are probably not sufficient reason for you to get into an altercation with the teacher, although you certainly should confer to iron out disagreements. A daily litany of substantial complaints, however, is cause for action. Your child has a right to expect your support; you should do all you can to remove her from a situation that could be damaging.

Sometimes the decisions you make in behalf of your child will be difficult. You may have to move out of your current school district to find a school system that's more accepting of gifted students. If you choose to stay where you are, you may be forced to continually advocate for your child. You may have to risk being labeled a "busybody" or a "pain in the neck." And you may end up having to go to court. Other parents have done so; their courage and perseverance have made it possible for their children—and others like them—to receive the kind of education they're entitled to. No matter what route you have to take, stay positive and polite. Don't get involved in name-calling and personal attacks. Keep your eye on the goal. You're teaching your child an important lesson—that he can count on you to be his best and strongest supporter.

Parent/Teacher Communication: Ways to Make it More Effective

There are two kinds of communication between teachers and parents—formal and informal. Formal communication consists of conferences and correspondence between home and school. Informal communication, which is often more valuable, occurs when parents participate in school activities and interact with teachers as friends and colleagues.

Formal communication can sometimes be a little threatening for one or the other participant. If a teacher calls a special conference, parents might feel intimidated; on the other hand, if parents ask for a conference, a teacher might feel defensive. These feelings arise because, when either a teacher or parent wants a conference, it's usually to deal with some problem, not simply for the parents to share how much Roberto loves school or for the teacher to gush over the child's accomplishments (although it would be delightful if there were more of these types of conferences).

If either parent or teacher requests a conference, here are some suggestions for making it more effective.

- *Listen first.*

Poor communication can result from entering into a discussion with preconceived notions about what the other person is going to say. You may, for example, think that the teacher is going to confront you about Roberto's talkativeness, and you go into the conference ready to defend him. How surprised you might be to find out that the teacher is concerned because Roberto is so quiet in class, and she's looking for suggestions on how she might draw him out!

- *Make eye contact.*

Eye contact ensures better listening. Remember that people open up when they think the listener is interested in what they have to say. Eye contact establishes a climate of interest and acceptance.

- *Wait before you respond.*

Sometimes people think they're listening when what they're really doing is preparing their response. If you want to be certain you've heard what the other person is saying, wait five seconds before you answer. The pause can help you be sure that the words you thought you heard were the words you really heard.

- *Paraphrase.*

Suppose a teacher says, "Bettina shouts out answers to questions before the other children have a chance to formulate a response." That's actually a pretty neutral statement, but you may interpret it to mean that the teacher thinks Bettina's too boisterous in class. Check out your impression with the teacher before you respond.

You might say, "If I hear you correctly, you're concerned that Bettina's too noisy." The teacher might then answer, "Oh, no, it's not the volume that's the issue. It's that she's so quick that the other children can't keep up. It's hard to get a class discussion going, because she knows the answers, and it's difficult for her to wait her turn to speak. Do you have some ideas about how we might gain her cooperation in giving others a chance?" Paraphrasing clarifies conversation and makes sure that both sides are talking about the same issue.

- *Stress "we," not "you."*

If the adults talk about what "we" or "all of us" can do to make the child's experience more positive, it helps eliminate finger-pointing and blame.

- *Show courtesy.*

Sometimes it's hard to be polite when you're hearing things that seem to reflect negatively on your parenting or teaching skills. Keep your focus on the problem, not your feelings. The five-second technique outlined earlier is particularly useful when you feel under attack. Waiting those five seconds to respond can keep you from saying something you might regret later.

- *Be sure to thank one another for taking the time to meet.*

Teachers have spouses and children, too, and conferences take many hours of personal or family time. Most parents also have jobs, and making time for a conference may mean a loss of vacation time. Be respectful of this time.

- *Control your emotions.*

There may be legitimate reasons for anger, sadness, or other emotions, but unless the case is exceptional, don't hold the conference when either one of you is very angry or upset. Wait to speak with one another until you've cooled down and collected your thoughts.

- *Keep an open mind.*

What works at home may not work at school; successful school strategies may fall flat at home. Enter the conference with the idea that you have things to learn from one another, rather than to push a specific agenda for the child.

- *Write a note of thanks to the teacher that summarizes the key points of your discussion and the decisions or agreements that were made.*

You may need documentation later if a teacher backs away from an agreed-upon strategy, or you may need proof that your child was accelerated or received some other type of curriculum option.

- *Understand that you will probably need more conferences.*

Seldom, if ever, can one conference resolve complex academic, emotional, and social issues. Finding the right "fit" or curriculum will be an ongoing concern.

In parent-teacher conferences, as in most other areas of life, a little sensitivity and tact go a long way in defusing what can be potentially difficult situations. Remember, too, that parents and teachers come from different perspectives.

Teachers in the early grades may have as many as thirty children in a class for a full day every day. In middle and high school, because classes change several times during the day, teachers may see several hundred students during the course of a year, and every year they deal with new young people. Although teachers are concerned about all of their students, it's unlikely that they will ever feel as deeply about a student as her parent or guardian does.

Nonetheless, teachers spend many hours each day with children and young people; their insights and instincts are usually keen and worthy of consideration. To work well together, parents and teachers need to know what's important to one another. Here are two lists of appreciations and suggestions gathered from parents and teachers.

Ten Things Parents Wish Teachers Knew

1. *I appreciate it when you recognize that my child doesn't need more of the same.* You create opportunities for my child to move at his own pace in areas in which he excels.

2. *I like it when you recognize that being gifted is only part of what (and who) my child is.* You don't constantly single out my child, in either a positive or negative light. You let him be a child first.

3. *I'm glad when you understand that my child will not excel in every area and you don't put pressure on her to measure up to unrealistic expectations.* Gifted children are unique and very different from one another. It pleases me when you recognize that she is more than a label and that to push her to be superior in every aspect of school life is detrimental to her social and emotional development.

4. *It makes me happy when you trust my child.* My gifted child likes being responsible for some of his own learning. When you trust my child to do inde-

pendent work, you're developing his self-discipline and confidence.

5. *It's satisfying when you communicate with me.* I want to know what strategies you're trying in the classroom and how they're working. In this way, I can build on and support your efforts in his education and development.

6. *I feel important when you treat me as a partner.* Not all teachers are trained in the intellectual, social, and emotional needs of gifted children. As a parent of one, I've made it my business to keep up with the research, and I appreciate it when you're open enough to understand that I have accumulated considerable knowledge about this subject.

7. *I appreciate that you don't discuss my child with other parents.* What is between you and me should stay between you and me. My child and I have a right to confidentiality, and I expect it.

8. *I'm not happy when you make assumptions about my parenting style.* If my child is behaving inappropriately at school, don't automatically assume that he behaves that way at home. Not every episode of bad behavior is a result of poor parenting. Share information about my child's behavior with me so we can solve the problem together.

9. *I'm frustrated when you automatically resist curriculum acceleration for my child based on her physical size, age, or other considerations that have nothing to do with her scholastic ability.* Long-term studies of gifted adults who were accelerated as children show that, despite age differences with their classmates, gifted students were popular and held leadership positions as often as children who weren't accelerated.

10. *I find it hard to feel comfortable with teachers who state that all children are gifted.* That makes as

much sense as saying that all children are mentally retarded. I agree that all children are special; each one is an individual to be valued and loved. I also agree that all children have various kinds of talents and abilities, and it's important to foster those talents. However, not every child has the advanced cognitive skills and capability that my child displays. She must be nurtured with accelerated individualized instruction and flexible educational options if she is to thrive and excel.

Ten Things Teachers Wish Parents Knew

1. *I appreciate it when you don't try to schedule a conference during the first two weeks of the school year.* The first ten days of school, I'm busy learning students' names, scheduling everything from mainstreaming to lunch and playground duties, getting to know new teaching or administrative staff members, and managing a multitude of other essential tasks. It's not the best time for an in-depth conversation.

2. *I like it when you show respect for me in front of your child.* If you ever have concerns about me or my teaching techniques, please bring them to my attention privately, rather than telling your child that her teacher "doesn't know what she's doing." Those kinds of statements give your child tacit permission to disobey me, ignore class rules, and behave inappropriately in my classroom.

3. *I'm gratified when you get your information first hand, not from other parents.* If you have a question about what's going on in the classroom, please ask me or come in and observe for a while. Stories children relate about classroom incidents can become

wildly inflated and inaccurate; if they are then repeated from parent to parent without verification, a teacher can very easily be maligned for something that simply didn't happen.

4. *I can feel more confident in our ability to work together when I know that you will keep our conversations private.* If you share our discussions with your child, you might misinterpret what I said or quote me out of context. Both can be harmful to your child.

5. *I appreciate that you understand that I have many children in my classroom.* As your child's teacher, I do my best every day to see that she receives the extension, enrichment, and reinforcement she needs. I appreciate your understanding that I also have to make sure other children with special needs are served, and that students who aren't as able as yours don't fail due to lack of my attention.

6. *I'm happy when I see you participating in school life.* When I know you better through informal meetings, I understand your child better. Seeing you just twice a year at a mandatory conference doesn't build a close relationship between us.

7. *I'm pleased when you respect my private property.* If you are volunteering in my classroom in an area where grade books and files are kept, I appreciate your knowing that those documents are off limits to everyone but me.

8. *It's wonderful when you provide enrichment for your child at home.* Learning takes place in school, out of school, on weekends, and during the summer. Education is everyone's job, and anything you can do to widen your child's experience brings a new dimension to the lessons I plan every day.

9. *I'm delighted when you treat me as a partner.* I'm glad to listen to your opinions on what we together

can do to give your child the best education possible. If you have relevant articles or books to share with me, please do so.

10. *I'm frustrated and annoyed when you try to dictate how I should do my job.* There are certain aspects of teaching that you cannot understand unless you've been a teacher yourself—in my school, with my students, and in my exact circumstances. There are a great many mandates in education today, not the least of which is the expectation that all children pass state proficiency examinations. There are certain policies and procedures that I must follow, and I may not be able to alter them as often as you think I can. Please have some trust and confidence in me.

Teamwork means listening, seeing the other's point of view, being respectful and sensitive toward one another, and expressing appreciation. These actions will foster the kind of cooperation necessary to help gifted children achieve the success they deserve.

Chapter 13

Questions and Answers

Question: *My son's teacher says that my son is restless in class and that he daydreams a lot. She has suggested that perhaps he might have ADHD (Attention Deficit Hyperactivity Disorder). I admit that sometimes I think she might be right. How can I tell whether his behavior is related to ADHD or is simply part of his giftedness (which has been confirmed by a battery of tests)?*

Answer: Of course it's possible that your son could be both gifted and ADHD, just as a child can be gifted and behaviorally handicapped or gifted and learning disabled. On the other hand, his attention could be wandering because he is bored, or he could just be exhibiting some of the psychomotor restlessness that may accompany giftedness. Here are some questions to ask yourself to help you sort the matter out:[39]

- Can your child sit still and concentrate on a task or activity other than television or computer games for an extended period of time?
- Does he have goals and a plan of action to make them happen?

[39]Webb, J. T. & Latimer, D. (1993). *ADHD and children who are gifted.* ERIC EC Digest (E522). Reston, VA: The Council for Exceptional Children.

- Does he work consistently in situations where he is intellectually stimulated?
- Does he set high standards in his areas of interest and work hard to meet them?
- Is there disagreement among the significant adults in the child's life about his behavior? That is, does the child behave differently in different circumstances—school, church, after-school activities?

If you answered "yes" to most of these questions, it's likely that your gifted child is simply acting the way many gifted children act. That is, his problems with staying on-task or completing assignments are probably due to his lack of interest or insufficient challenge in specific curriculum areas, not ADHD. But if you are still in doubt and concerned, it might be helpful for him to complete other kinds of psychological tests for ADHD and for emotional distress, and also to have a thorough physical examination just to be sure there are no hidden causes for his disruptive behavior in the classroom or elsewhere.

If, after careful observation and testing, your child is determined to suffer from ADHD, there are many strategies that can be tried to help him focus for longer periods. Your child's school psychologist, pediatrician, and classroom teacher can all help.

But if factors other than giftedness are ruled out, it's time to confer with the teacher about classroom behaviors, bringing the test results with you. Try to be part of a learning experience for your child's teacher. Ask questions about your child's actions throughout the school day. Share knowledge and propose strategies politely. Ask the teacher's opinion, and be sure to give the teacher a chance to respond.

Behavioral strategies can often help children learn to concentrate on tasks, ignore distractions, and be less impulsive. Sometimes a simple behavior contract similar to the learning contracts he might use in school can be of use. The one that follows is an example.

Sample Behavior Contract

I, Bruce McGraw, agree to finish my math homework every evening by 8:00 p.m.. I will check to see that each problem is answered completely, and I will do my best to solve the problems accurately.

We, Robert and/or Jeanne McGraw, agree to be available between 7:00 p.m. and 8:00 p.m. to check math homework for completeness. We will not check problems for accuracy, because accuracy is Bruce's responsibility. We will, however, explain concepts to the best of our ability.

If Bruce completes his math homework by 8:00 p.m., he will be entitled to play computer games for one half hour, between 8:00 and 8:30 p.m. If his homework is not completed, we will not intervene. He will receive consequences imposed by his teacher.

Signed: Bruce McGraw   Date: _____
          Robert McGraw   _____
          Jeanne McGraw   _____

Question: *My child's teacher is so busy that he never seems have time to talk with me. I've dropped in at lunch hour, recess, and after school, and he always seems very rushed.*

Answer: You will have much better luck if you schedule a conference. Your child's teacher cannot be prepared to answer your questions or to speak with you in-depth if he doesn't know you're coming. "Dropping in" is all right if you just want to pick up a homework assignment for your sick child or return a book, but don't expect the teacher to be able to put aside all other work or give up his lunch whenever you drop by. After school, the teacher may be rushed because he has an appointment or needs to pick up his own children. Please be as considerate of the teacher's schedule as you would want him to be of yours.

Question: *My daughter has been identified as gifted, but her teacher says that all the children in her class have various gifts, and she needs to tend to every one. I am so concerned, and my daughter's behavior is starting to take a nosedive.*

Answer: Your child's teacher is clearly dedicated to bringing out the best in every child, but it's possible that she may be referring to the theory of multiple intelligences rather than to giftedness.

The theory of multiple intelligences formulated by Howard Gardner in 1983 helps explain that children often learn in quite different ways. Gardner believes that there are eight intelligences: linguistic, logical-mathematical, visual-spatial, bodily-kinesthetic, musical, intrapersonal, interpersonal, and naturalistic. Each child has all eight of these intelligences, but some areas are more developed than others. For example, some children grasp mathematical concepts most easily through discussion. Others need to feel and manipulate objects, mathematical models, shapes, and numbers. Some children learn best in a group; others are more comfortable with pen-and-pencil work they do alone. In most classrooms today, teachers use a variety of instructional methods to engage students' different styles of learning.

Whatever their learning style, however, gifted children learn faster than other students. They need greater depth and breadth in their educational experience. Even if a teacher is perfectly matching activities to the gifted child's preferred learning style, the student is not receiving the kind of learning challenges that she requires if the curriculum is not being expanded and accelerated.

Here's an analogy you might try with your child's teacher to help her understand. Suppose a child is eight years old and can play "Twinkle, Twinkle Little Star" on the violin. Suppose another child is seven years old and can play a violin concerto well enough to receive an invitation to play with a local orchestra. Should the seven-year-old be held back, forced to play "Twinkle, Twinkle Little Star" over and over because that's what all of the other children can play?

In the example, both children have musical talent, but that's where the similarity ends. One is gifted—perhaps highly gifted—and one is not. The one who is gifted requires special accommodation for her high ability and performance.

In his excellent article, "Aren't All Children Athletic?"[40] James R. Delisle argues convincingly for differentiated education. "Do we

---
[40] Delisle, J. R. (1991, February 27). *Education Week*, Commentary.

ever hear the same hue and cry," he says, "when … a coach selects a small number of children for a starting spot on the varsity squad? Of course we don't, for we recognize the validity of placing children together with others … with similarly refined athletic skills."

All of the children in your daughter's class have various types of talents, and the teacher should find ways to enrich *every* child's experience, including your gifted daughter's.

Question: I think my daughter would benefit from whole grade acceleration. She tested far above the average on all achievement tests, and the school psychologist has found her ability to be exceptional. She is very mature, tall for her age, popular, well-adjusted, and comfortable with older students. I'd like to speak with the teachers and administrators at school about whole grade acceleration. How would you suggest that I proceed?

Answer: Ask your school or district if they have available the *Iowa Acceleration Scale*. If they do, request that it be used for your child to determining if whole grade acceleration is appropriate. If not, suggest that they obtain it. This research-based tool offers systematic guidance in this area and helps educators and parents consider each factor that is important for successful whole grade acceleration. A whole grade acceleration based on such a thoughtful and systematic approach is generally quite successful. However, other options, such as single subject acceleration or a mentorship, might also be appropriate. Whichever is determined to be the best solution for your daughter, include the receiving teacher in all discussions since she needs to be an important part of the planning process.

Question: My son's teacher is expanding the curriculum only slightly for him. He still must study every subject at the same time as the other students, and it's mostly lectures and worksheets. My son is very unhappy. The teacher is quite honest about the fact that she's "teaching to the test," because there's such an emphasis on the children doing well on the state proficiency exams. What should we do? The teacher and I have already had several conferences.

Answer: "Teaching to the test" is an unfortunate side effect of state proficiency examinations. Passing the tests is extremely important to educators, because teachers' and administrators' salaries, advancement, and job security often depend on how well their students do on the test.

One way you might engage the cooperation of the teacher and the administration is by helping them understand that if they allow gifted students more opportunities to excel, it's these students who will raise the test scores and make their schools and teachers look very good indeed. The school's self-interest is clearly served by providing the best students with all the tools they need to perform up to their potential.

Ask the teacher if there are independent activities your son can do to expand his experience. If the class is studying the planets, for example, ask the teacher if the child can write a special report on his visit to the planetarium or do some Internet research at home on black holes. Most teachers won't refuse independent work if it doesn't create additional preparation time and hardship for them. As a concerned parent, you can also provide a great deal of encouragement and enrichment at home to supplement your son's school learning. Have your son bring home projects or research he would like to do, and then set aside some evening time for him to work on it with you.

Question: My son is capable of a great deal scholastically, but he's getting Ds and an occasional F. How can I help him climb out of this pattern of underachievement?

Answer: Begin with a visit to the doctor for a thorough physical examination, including a careful check of his hearing and vision. Sometimes a child who cannot see well doesn't even realize that his vision is poor, because he's never seen any other way or because his eyesight has been worsening incrementally over a long period of time. Emotional problems, such as depression, can also affect the ability to perform adequately. Examine the possibility that your son's underachievement and low grades are part of a somewhat disguised power struggle between you and your son or your son and his teacher.

After making sure that your son is physically and emotionally healthy, you may want to read about underachievement. There are several books available for parents of children who underachieve. One is Sylvia Rimm's *Why Bright Children Get Poor Grades: And What You Can Do About It*. Rimm discusses in detail how underachievement is related to perfectionism, family dynamics, school expectations, and more. *Guiding the Gifted Child* by James Webb, Elizabeth Meckstroth and Stephanie Tolan also contains a great deal of helpful information about lack of motivation and other reasons for underachievement.

Question: I'm thinking of home-schooling my gifted daughter, because our school district doesn't have what she needs. I'm reticent to do it, however, because I worry about her socialization. She's a bit shy, and I can see her becoming a complete loner if there aren't other children around. What should I do?

Answer: Home-schooling of gifted children is growing in popularity. If you are capable of being your child's teacher; enriching her experience with field trips, mentors, and independent projects; and also fulfilling your state's curricular and legal requirements, then home-schooling might be something for you to try.

Home-schooling parents need support, and you may be able to find a group of parents who meet for this purpose. Check out Web sites for home-schooling gifted children in your state. The landscape of home-schooling is changing so rapidly that new groups and programs are popping up every day. Some organizations will help you design your curriculum and provide guidance and testing materials.

Although the outlook for home-schooling is positive, home-schooling is not right for every child, nor is it the best choice for every parent. Some parents don't have the time, energy, or patience to home-school successfully, and if both parents work outside the home, the home-schooling option becomes nearly impossible.

You are right that children need peers and playmates, and as your child's home teacher, you will have to create opportunities for her to play and socialize with other children on a regular basis.

Some school districts allow home-schooled children to participate in co-curricular activities such as music, or to attend school part-time. Check with your local district or state Department of Education.

Weigh the pros and cons carefully, be honest about your own strengths and weaknesses, and discuss the idea with others who have tried it, as well as with your child.

Question: My son's teacher told me that he is an overachiever. What does this mean?

Answer: If an underachiever is someone whose level of achievement is lower than would be predicted, based on the person's observed abilities and talents, what is overachievement? What most people call overachievement could also be called over-striving—that is, trying too hard to be the best at everything and never taking time to rest, relax, or just enjoy life. It's an aspect of perfectionism, and overstrivers may be workaholics-in-training. Parents can try to attack the problem at its root, using strategies that help the child understand that perfection is impossible.

Of course this must be kept in perspective. As Jane Piirto says in her book *Talented Children and Adults,* "How can a person achieve more than they [sic] can achieve? The attention to mediocrity, to fitting in, to getting by, to not rocking the boat, all feed into the concept of overachievement. [Society says] the talented student … should let up a little, should fit in a little, should not have such high standards." In other words, the culture teaches talented children to give less than their best or risk ostracism and jealousy from other, less capable, students. What a difficult quandary for a bright, talented child! So perhaps your son is not an overachiever after all.

Question: Is it common to have more than one gifted child?

Answer: Linda Silverman of the Gifted Development Center in Denver, Colorado, says in an article on the center's Web site that if one child in the family is identified as gifted, there is a substantially greater chance that siblings will be gifted as well.[41] Her

---

[41]Silverman, L. (1999). *What have we learned about gifted children,* 1979-1999. Denver, CO: Gifted Development Center.

research indicates that ability test scores of brothers and sisters are usually within five to ten points of one another. However, second-born children are less likely than first-borns to be recognized as gifted.

Remember that even if siblings are gifted, they may be gifted in entirely different ways and have totally different types of personalities. Also, siblings often take on completely different roles within the family, such as the comedian, the athlete, the socialite, or even the underachiever. Every child wants to be recognized for something, and if the oldest is a high-achieving, straight A student, the next sibling may choose a "field" other than academics in which to excel.

Question: *I'm almost afraid to ask this question, because nobody believes me when I talk about it. I have a seven-month-old baby, and she's started to talk. Not complete sentences, but recognizable words—"mama," "doggy," and most surprising to me, "banana" and "sunshine." Am I crazy or could this really be happening?*

Answer: It's unusual, but also quite possible. The research on gifted children mentions many children like yours. Some of the characteristics associated with highly gifted children include:[42]

- Early language development (the mean age at which most of these children spoke their first word is nine months, which means that some spoke earlier).
- Unusual alertness in infancy.
- A long attention span in infancy and toddlerhood.
- A need for less sleep than other children.

You may be a little frightened by what is clearly one indication of giftedness. Don't panic. As your daughter grows, you'll get a more complete picture. If she is a profoundly gifted child, you will need help in keeping up with her rapid learning.

---

[42]Rogers, K. & Silverman, L. (1997, January). *A study of 241 profoundly gifted children.* Paper presented at the National Association for Gifted Children 44th Annual Convention, Little Rock, AR.

Begin now to read books and magazine articles on giftedness. The World Wide Web has many sites that deal with giftedness. Start with the Web site for the National Association for Gifted Children (www.nagc.org), which offers links to many others.

The Gifted Development Center does a great deal of research in the field of highly gifted children, and you can find interesting articles on its Web site (www.gifteddevelopment.org). Conferring with experts or reading good books in the field can help you sort out the issues you may be facing in the future.

Question: *We have just moved to the city where my parents live, but we know few other people right now. My mother and my gifted daughter share many interests. Are family members good mentors for children?*

Answer: Grandparents can be exceptional mentors. In general, unless they're a negative influence, grandparents are just plain good for their grandchildren. Because they're removed from the daily hurly-burly of living with children, grandparents can be more patient. They have more unstructured time to listen, work on projects or puzzles, read aloud, listen to music, play games, and tell stories. They have a longer perspective and can provide interesting insights on how life used to be and how it is today. Children generally love stories of the days when Grandma was in school.

In addition, Grandma and Grandpa can provide a day—or more—of respite for both parents and children. The children return home refreshed to well-rested parents. It's a win-win-win for everyone.

Question: *My son is so proud of himself for being "gifted" that he seems to think he should be excused from all the mundane household duties that his mother, his siblings, and I complete as a matter of course. How can I bring him back to reality?*

Answer: It's time to have a private chat with your son, asking him to explain why he thinks high scholastic ability should exempt him from "membership" in the family. This discussion should be dispassionate rather than emotional. Ask him to discuss the possible effects his behavior has on the other members of the family. Can he see that when he refuses to do his part, others must pick up the slack? Is this fair to the others? How does he think this will affect his relationship with his siblings over the long term?

Set firm behavioral guidelines. Within these limits, give choices. The real world will not give your son a free pass, and he needs to learn that now. In Rudolf Dreikurs' book, *Children: The Challenge*, family meetings are suggested as a way to resolve issues like this. Dreikurs also describes many other techniques, such as logical and natural consequences. Using some of these approaches will help your son appreciate the effects of his behavior.

Question: What are the benefits of creative problem-solving programs for gifted children? My daughter has shown some interest in Future Problem Solving, *but I don't know much about it.*

Answer: Creative problem-solving programs, such as *Future Problem Solving, Destination ImagiNation*, and *Invent America* can be useful for children in many ways. First, these programs require that children work together to solve problems; that aspect of the programs helps gifted children sharpen their skills in both teamwork and leadership. Second, to solve the problems, they have to call on their higher order thinking skills and resourcefulness, and sometimes they have to fail in order to learn. Failure on the way to success is a good lesson for perfectionistic students. When the students finally arrive at creative solutions that work, their self-confidence is enhanced.

The whole process of solving complex problems can be very liberating for gifted children, because to come up with creative solutions, they get to "think outside the box." This kind of wide-ranging thinking comes easily for most gifted students. They feel at home and comfortable dealing with complicated issues. According to the Web site of the *Future Problem Solving* program (www.fpsp.org), the mission is "to teach students how to think, not what to think." Other similar programs have the same emphasis. Most of the programs have some degree of competitiveness; the national competitions of students involved with Invent America have attracted considerable media attention.

Your daughter may benefit from participating in a creative problem-solving program. Make her aware, however, that these activities require time and effort, and other students in her group will be counting on her to do her share.

Question: I need some quick ideas to help my son deal with stress. He knows when he's becoming overstressed, but he doesn't know what to do about it. What do you suggest?

Answer: It's great that your son is in tune with his stress levels, and it's wonderful that you're in a position to help. Here are some suggestions.

- *Change the environment.* If stress comes when he's studying or preparing for tests, remind him to take regular study breaks. Encourage him to use those breaks to play a game, get some exercise, play with a pet, or "veg out" for a few minutes.

- *Give him permission to "decompress."* Allow time for him to talk about the stresses in his life. You don't have to solve his problems for him; just listen. If he asks for your opinion, feel free to share it, but otherwise don't get dragged into the situation. Taking on your child's worries and concerns can greatly raise your own stress level, and at that point, you lose your value as an objective listener.

- *Help him learn to set limits.* Your child has a finite amount of energy. Teach him how to say no to activities and projects that will drain him and provide no particular benefit. You may have to set some limits for the child as well. Some children become so engrossed in a topic or activity that they do it to the exclusion of everything else. The parent must then step in to ensure that the child has a more well-rounded experience of life.

- *See that he has sufficient physical activity.* Exercise is one of nature's great stress relievers. Encourage it and participate in it yourself. Walking or jogging together benefits your health and provides a stress-free environment for conversation.

- *Teach him to concentrate on and finish one thing at a time.* Gifted children often get involved in many areas at once, with the result that nothing gets done very well. Unfinished projects, neglected homework, and last-minute hurrying are typical behaviors for students who have difficulty staying with one thing for very long.

Some parents swear by the martial arts, such as tae kwan do or karate, to help children learn to focus. These activities provide physical exercise and require that students be disciplined and centered throughout the lesson. The ability to concentrate then carries over into their intellectual work. Martial arts also provide a structured reward system that can help children make the connection between effort and accomplishment. In addition, students who feel in control of their bodies may become more confident and assured in general.

Question: For some reason, my daughter panics over homework. Do you have any ideas about what is happening and what to do about it?

Answer: Do you know specifically what's causing her anxiety? Ask her to pinpoint what upsets her most, and work just on that one issue. It will also be helpful to establish a homework routine. Having a specific time and place to do homework makes it easier for students to get to work quickly. Some students like to start with the hardest work first. Then they can coast through the remaining assignments. Other students prefer to do easier work first. The feeling of success motivates them to move on to the more challenging subjects. Ask your daughter which way she likes to work, and help her organize her tasks accordingly.

Huge reading assignments can overwhelm even gifted students. Show your daughter how to use preview questions and chapter subheadings to guide her comprehension.

Students sometimes take such copious class notes that by the time they get home, they can't make sense of them. It's far better for students to listen to the lecture itself, taking notes only when they hear an important point. Outline notes are very helpful, because many teachers present lectures in outline form, with main points supported by sub-points. The more your daughter listens, the more she'll understand. You may want to help her practice at home by having her listen to you read a short newspaper article, then find the key points and put them into an outline.

Question: I have two sons, ages three and four, who seem to fit many of the criteria for giftedness, and I am totally exhausted! If I don't keep them busy every minute, they are into everything. Help!

Answer: Parenting two small gifted children is bound to be exhausting! Be sure to read the story of hope in the next chapter to find out how one mother created an environment for learning in her home. You must be committed to enriching your boys' lives as much as possible; their energy levels are no doubt very high, and that energy needs to be channeled. Take them with you to as many places as you reasonably can to expand their experience of the world.

At home, create a space where the boys' activities can be relatively unrestricted, and stock that area with art materials (washable, of course!), puzzles and games, kitchen equipment, blocks and other building materials, Lego™ sets or other construction toys, sheets for building forts and castles, home-made costumes for role-playing, and of course, books. Haunt garage sales (and take the boys with you); you'll find many wonderful, virtually unused books and games at one-tenth the price you would pay for them in a store.

Talk with your sons, read to them, and provide them with opportunities to both listen to music and make their own. Take them to the library for story hour and to select their own books.

Make sure they have adequate physical outlets for their high spirits. A simple game of tag has many advantages: they're playing together, they're outside exercising, and they're discharging some of their energy. Sometimes a tired child is exactly what a parent needs most!

Give them responsibilities. Three- and four-year-olds can learn to do simple household chores such as sorting laundry, setting the table, and picking up their own toys and games.

Of course, the children need rest, too, and most children, including gifted ones, are comforted by routines. Have consistent rest periods and bedtime. If the children are especially energetic in the evenings, it's very important to give them a relatively lengthy quiet period before bed, for conversation, reading, or looking at books.

If the boys aren't in preschool, now may be a good time to look for one. Gifted children need opportunities to socialize with other children so they can begin to learn early how to relate to others.

Many of the resources on the *Learn More About ...* pages at the end of this book have very good strategies for dealing effectively with the curiosity, high energy levels, and frequent emotionalism of gifted children.

Question: Do minority (African American, Hispanic, Asian, or Native American) gifted children sometimes have greater feelings of isolation that their Anglo counterparts?

Answer: A report on giftedness in the African American community, researched by Donna Ford, concluded that African American students may feel greater isolation because: 1) they are under-represented in gifted programs and so are racially isolated from the white students in the program; 2) by being in the gifted program, they are isolated from the majority of students of their own race, some of whom may be actively hostile to anyone in such a program; 3) they may be estranged from their teachers if the teachers don't understand the issues of multiculturalism; and 4) they can be isolated from their own families, because some family members may not be familiar with what giftedness is and how it manifests itself. [43]

If African American children lack positive racial self-concepts, they are especially at risk when it comes to peer pressure, particularly if they are told by peers that participation in a gifted program means they are "acting white." Some students may begin to underachieve in order to stay affiliated with racial peers who are not involved in a gifted program.[44]

However, "not all African American children have problems being members of a gifted class," says Hank Griffith, Sr., a minority administrator in a large suburban school system. "Children from high-achieving families who go to schools beyond the urban center have less difficulty with peer pressure. Gifted students tend to accept other gifted students of any race, and parents with high expectations reinforce the idea that education and achievement are positive values."

Griffith also notes, however, that for children in the urban core, the picture may be far different. "These young people are often very happy in their gifted program, but after school is over, they have to go back to some mean streets—places where education is not valued and achievement is something to laugh at."

Griffith's comments clearly highlight that schools have a big responsibility, not only to these children, but also to their families. The gifted educators in city schools must reach out to parents, because the parents need to be comfortable with the idea of giftedness in order to make their child comfortable with it. If the parent doesn't support the child's inclusion in the gifted program, it's much harder for the child to succeed. A gifted child will be too vulnerable to peer pressure without a strong support system at home.

"Parents, grandparents, and other significant adults in the child's life," Griffith says, "have to be provided with the strategies to help him cope with a dual identity—one for school and one for the neighborhood. For example, some urban students actually *must* speak two very distinct kinds of English—correct English for

---

[43]Ford, D. Y. (1994). *The recruitment and retention of African American students in gifted education programs: Implications and recommendations* (RBDM 9406). Storrs, CT: The National Research Center on the Gifted and Talented, University of Connecticut.

[44]Ford, D. Y. (1997). *Underachievement among gifted minority students: Problems and promises.* ERIC Digest (E554). Reston, VA: The ERIC Clearinghouse on Disabilities and Gifted Education.

school and street slang for their peer group—if they're to maintain their standing in both places. Children can straddle the line effectively if they're given some practical help about ways to deal with out-of-school pressures, but the parents need the tools to help the child. Sometimes the best way to enrich children's lives may be to enrich their parents' lives. Schools can do that by helping parents understand their kids and giving the parents support as they try to raise their children under less than ideal circumstances."

Identity issues may also affect members of any ethnic or racial group as they strive to balance respect and observance of their own culture, language, and traditions with those of the majority. For example, recent immigrants who speak English as a second language may feel isolated both linguistically and socially. It's difficult and frustrating for bright students to try to demonstrate their gifts when they haven't yet mastered the language. That's why a multi-factored approach to identifying all gifted children is so critical.

The National Association for Gifted Children estimates that there are approximately three million gifted children in the United States, and that these children are members of every race, ethnicity, and socio-economic group. If we don't reach them all, that's a tragedy, because the world surely needs the talents of all its gifted citizens!

Chapter 14

Parent to Parent—A Story of Hope

Karen Rapp is the mother of Adrienne, a gifted daughter who is now an adult. Karen and Adrienne's story encompasses many aspects of giftedness and ranges from Adrienne's babyhood to her upcoming graduation from college. Karen was willing (with Adrienne's permission) to share her story to bring other parents a picture of what life with a gifted child has been like for her. Adrienne's story illustrates some of the highs and lows of dealing with giftedness and should bring hope to many parents who are struggling to make sense of events or behaviors that might be happening in their own children's lives.

There is one particularly dramatic episode in Adrienne's story—her recovery from a life-threatening illness. Although Karen believes that her daughter's strong mind was paramount in her return to health, it is imperative that parents not try to cure illness solely with positive thinking or the power of the mind. Critically ill children need specialized care, which Adrienne received from both her personal physician and a dedicated hospital staff.

Karen's Story

Adrienne was born after a wonderful pregnancy. It was an easy birth, and she was an absolutely adorable little girl. I thought I was the perfect mom because she was the perfect child. I later discovered that neither was true, but it was fun while it lasted; she was completely delightful as a baby and toddler. I didn't realize that she had special talents for quite a while because I was the first of my friends to have a child. With no other babies to compare her to, I thought she was just bright, and I was certainly happy about that.

Looking back now, I can see that she was always advanced. When she was just a year old, I often took her with me when I played tennis with my friends. She would sit very contentedly in her portable swing, turning the pages in a book, one by one. I could play tennis for an hour and she'd never make a peep. It was great for me, and she seemed to enjoy it, too.

I could take her out to lunch with me, and she would read her books and behave perfectly. In fact, I could take her anywhere I went; she was always able to amuse herself.

The fact that she could entertain herself so well was a big clue that she was unusual. Even when she was just able to sit up—at about six months—I could put her down on a blanket, put her toys around her, and she'd be just fine. Of course, I did lots of things with her because I was an at-home mom, but if I needed to get my own work done, I knew she would stay in one place and be okay by herself.

It was a neighbor who first pointed out to me that Adrienne was very young to be able to match the blocks in her shape-sorter box. She could do that at six months.

She also had an advanced understanding of concepts. When she was two, her favorite playmate was the little boy next door. One day she came home early from playing because he was being punished for something. She looked up at me and said, "Mrs. Smith shouldn't punish Mitchell, because she's punishing me, too. Now I don't have anyone to play with."

When she was quite young, she also criticized *my* parenting. "I think that's too harsh a punishment for what I did," she would sometimes say. One evening a few years later, she sat down with one of the parenting books I was reading and highlighted all the things she thought it was important for parents to do. I thought, "Oh my goodness, what am I dealing with here?"

When she was three or four, Adrienne had an imaginary playmate named Jenny. Although she never described Jenny to me, and I didn't have to set a place at the dinner table for Jenny, Adrienne talked to her all the time in her room during naps and at bedtime. She would never speak to Jenny when the rest of the family was around, but I could sometimes hear her having whole conversations with her imaginary friend. They were word-for-word replays of talks she and I had had earlier in the day, only Adrienne would take my role and Jenny apparently took on Adrienne's part. Jenny disappeared when Adrienne started elementary school.

A Delightful Handful

My understanding about Adrienne's unusual intelligence came initially from other people. At the end of first grade, her teacher asked me if I'd like to go over her test scores. We were very busy building a house at the time, and I'd forgotten that she'd taken some IQ tests at school. Her teacher told me that Adrienne had an extremely high score. That was the first confirmation I had that she might be a little bit brighter than the other children.

As she got older, it was increasingly difficult for me to stay ahead of her, and it took a huge amount of energy just to keep up. I was really glad I wasn't working outside my home, because she truly was a full-time job. When Adrienne's brother and sister came along, I had to spend a lot of time organizing and planning things to keep them all busy.

It was fortunate that they were self-motivated children who found things to do on their own, but I always felt that I needed to keep providing opportunities for them because they were all very willing to try just about anything. We took little educational trips and toured museums. Adrienne always said that we saw so many museums, she'd never step foot in another one. However, when she went to Europe last year, she hit the museums in all of the countries she visited.

But we didn't just do museums on our educational trips. We'd also take time out for ice cream or a dip at the pool. We always had a whole schedule of activities. I tried to make it fun, but at the same time provide as many opportunities for learning as I could.

Adrienne was the type of child who, when we went on vacation, would organize and entertain the other children. When we went to the lake, the children would go outside every morning, and I wouldn't see them again for the rest of the day. She would have all the kids from the other cabins doing obstacle courses on the beach or building sand animals. Her creativity and leadership were just astounding.

When she got a little older and babysat for her brother and sister, that same creativity was evident. We'd go out for dinner and when we'd come back, the basement would be transformed into a castle or a school or a skyscraper or something else. Sheets would be draped here and there; backdrops would be painted. The whole scene would be in place, and the kids would be acting out a story.

With all the artistic creation going on, we had to restrict the children to the basement; otherwise the house would have been covered with paint and glitter. The basement was theirs, however. They could do what they wanted to down there, including drawing on the walls. The basement wasn't finished and they really couldn't hurt anything.

Life in Elementary School

I have to say that, in general, Adrienne's teachers were supportive of her. I remember one teacher in particular who told me that when he did a whole-class lesson, all he could ever see was the top of Adrienne's head. As he walked down the aisle one day, he discovered that she had a book on her lap and that she always read during his classroom presentations. "If it were anyone but Adrienne," he said, "I'd put a stop to it, but I know she can handle both reading and listening at the same time, so I leave her alone."

Some teachers, however, weren't as helpful. One teacher told me that Adrienne's test scores from the previous year couldn't possibly be as high as they were, because "we just don't see children here who are that bright." When I asked her if she'd ever looked at Adrienne's school record, she said she hadn't. I became annoyed; she had made all of these assumptions without even knowing Adrienne.

In frustration, I said, "Would you please review her record to make sure I haven't misinterpreted her scores and what the other teachers have said?" Once this teacher looked, she ended up following the recommendations of the previous teachers by giving Adrienne more advanced reading and math. Until she did so, however, it was a struggle to get her to acknowledge Adrienne's capabilities. It was frustrating to be told that what I knew to be true *couldn't* be true.

Adrienne was very bonded to the kids in her gifted magnet program. It was a place where *everyone* was different, and the students accepted one another's differences. Relationships were extremely important to her because she was so sensitive. She was either very up or very down, and she was easily depressed. Her magnet class friends were lifesavers to her because they understood her. In that class, she didn't always have to conform. Her gifted teacher was good at letting the kids come through as their own true selves. That wasn't true in other classes, where teachers were sometimes intimidated by gifted students.

In the magnet class, the kids could go off in their own directions and experiment with their own ideas. There were stations everywhere for different kinds of work, and they got to help plan their own assignments. They could choose topics from a list of options and decide with the teacher how they were going to work on them. Unlike other classrooms, they didn't have a choice of only two formats and one method of presentation. It gave them a sense of control over their lives.

Life Outside of School

Adrienne was always enthusiastically involved in activities outside of school. She took dance and piano lessons, and then she *really* got into gymnastics. She started winning all these little trophies, and she had fun doing that. It was an outlet for her, which was great, because she needed a place where she was kept busy. When she came home in the evenings, if she didn't have something going on, she would drive us crazy.

Adrienne was like a motor running constantly. When she was in the house, everything tended to be focused and centered on her. There was an actual difference in the atmosphere of the house when she was there. She wore us out, and the older she got, the more exhausting she became to parent. I don't mean that in a negative way; she just consumed a lot of my time and energy. So, in some ways, it was nice to have her in the gym four hours a night, because when she got home, she was tired. Even then, though, she didn't completely run down.

In the fourth and fifth grade, after she would come in from the gym, she would want to talk and talk. I would sit beside her as she got everything off her chest. She had to do that before she could go to sleep. A couple of times, I actually fell asleep listening to her because I really didn't have to participate in the conversation. She only wanted a warm body beside her to listen to her and care about her. Rarely did I ever say a word. With her sensitivity, she didn't want me to give an opinion or criticize.

To this day, she still likes to work out her own problems. She wants to discuss them with me, but she doesn't want advice or comments.

A Reason for Concern

Adrienne is a deep and talented thinker and writer, and in middle school, her writings became frightening. Some of her poetry was very depressing and heavy. In one of the poems, the narrator ended up walking into the ocean. I wondered if these poems were expressions of how she was feeling; they were almost suicidal. I asked her gifted teacher to look them over because they were scaring me. Did Adrienne want to walk into a black hole? Her teacher explained that some of what I was reading had to do with Adrienne's developmental level, which in some ways was already like an older adolescent's.

I called a librarian friend who was active with middle-schoolers. She told me that middle school kids sometimes write stories and poems like this, but that Adrienne's were exaggerated. The subject matter wasn't unusual, but her stories were a little extreme. I also sent the stories to her pediatrician to look at. He said that they actually were a good outlet for her, but that I should be alert for personality changes or alterations in her daily activities.

Adrienne always journaled. She wrote about things that happened at school, in her relationships, and what was going on between the two of us. The journals, too, were very intense.

In High School

By the time Adrienne got to high school, she'd been in club gymnastics for years. She went to school, went to the gym, came home, did homework, and went to bed. She wasn't having much fun. Her class load was heavy because she was taking a number of AP courses. She decided she'd like to have more friends and a better time at school.

By the time she was a junior, she continued to take honors courses, though she lightened up on the number, and she switched from club gymnastics to the school gymnastics team. She tried out for cheerleading. She took Accounting I because a lot of "fun guys" were in the class; she didn't find the course particularly challenging, but she had such a good time that she went on to take Accounting II.

Adrienne was one of the youngest in her high school class and one of the smallest as well. That was a bit of a problem, because while academically she was far ahead, socially she had some growing up to do. Although she loved being a cheerleader, she didn't like a lot of the social pressures that went with it. She felt that she didn't quite fit anywhere; the social whirl was a little confusing. She tried to play the game, but sometimes it was hard for her.

A Life-Threatening Illness and the Power of the Mind

Although Adrienne is very gifted, she doesn't always show a lot of common sense. She pushes herself too hard. She feels invincible and doesn't see the connections between things like getting enough sleep and maintaining her health. When she sees something she wants to do, she does it without a lot of thought about the possible consequences to herself.

At the end of Adrienne's freshman year of college it became apparent that she'd been overextended—taking a heavy course load, tutoring, having an active social life, making excellent grades, and holding down a job. Because of her extraordinary energy and will, she was able to do all of these things, but she didn't realize the toll they were taking on her. Due to her gymnastics training, she was physically strong. She just wasn't aware of how her health was suffering. She picked up the mono virus, which slowed her down a bit.

When I looked at her one morning, I said, "You look awful. Your skin is yellow." She was determined that she was going to go to work, but I convinced her to wait until I spoke with the doctor.

When we discovered that the whites of her eyes had also turned yellow, I called the doctor to get an immediate appointment. He thought it was hepatitis, but we needed blood tests to confirm the diagnosis. We went to the hospital for the blood tests and then she went home to bed rather than to her job.

The doctor said that if she wasn't better in the morning, he would hospitalize her and give her IVs to get her rehydrated. She wasn't better the next morning. In fact, everything was pretty much falling apart; we just didn't know it yet. We took her back to the hospital, and while she was getting the hydrating IVs, the staff kept drawing more blood. Her first blood test results were starting to come back in, and it was apparent that something was very wrong. The doctor made arrangements for her immediate transfer to Children's Hospital.

By the time we got her there, she was so weak that she could hardly get in the door. We were losing her, and she was admitted to the Emergency Department right away.

Adrienne became semi-conscious. The doctors and nurses seemed to be alarmed and were really rushing around. They didn't know precisely what was causing her symptoms, but everything in her body was starting to fail. Her blood pressure was dropping, she was in acute kidney failure, she had hepatitis, her blood cells were attacking each other, and she wasn't making any red cells. She was paper white.

I was in shock. At one point, she looked at me and said, "Am I going to die?" I didn't know how to respond. My sister was on her way, the doctor was on his way, but there was no one with me at the time.

I decided I had to answer her question, though, so I went to the head of her bed and whispered, "Adrienne, you have a really strong mind. You have a lot of power in your mind. You have to use it now. You have to start thinking about your body and commanding it to function. That's your job. You don't have to do anything else."

I'd read some things on mental imaging, so I tried to help her create healing images. I told her to get the "good guys" into her body, from the top of her head down to her toes. They could be anything she wanted—gymnasts, Pac Men, or musicians—but they had to get to work. I told her I would be right there, thinking along with her, and that she would get over this. "You have to help all of us," I said. "And you have to do it right now."

Finally, the nurse said, "We need to put Adrienne on life support to assist her breathing. It will take twenty minutes to make all the preparations." I told them that they could prep her, but I refused to allow the life support until her doctor arrived. When he got there about ten minutes later, I decided that he could handle the medical decisions, and I would devote my efforts solely to Adrienne. I sat by her head and asked, "Are you thinking?"

The doctor decided that Adrienne didn't need life support. Fifteen minutes later she was getting a blood transfusion, and her color got better. To this day, I'm not sure what really transpired in those ten or fifteen minutes, but she started to come back.

After three or four days, she got of out Intensive Care, but her kidneys still weren't working properly. So that became our focus. Her doctor and I wondered how to motivate her to think positively and concentrate on healing. She's never been the kind of person that you could just tell to work hard; you had to come up with something creative to engage her mind—something that had an impact on her and caught her attention. We had to get her to realize the seriousness of her kidney situation, because dialysis was the next step.

I asked, "Adrienne, if you could have one thing in your whole life, what would it be?" We were looking for anything to focus on that would give her a reason to want to get better.

She said, "You know, I've always wanted a Jeep."

"Okay," we said, "if you can focus on having normal kidney chemistry levels, you'll be that much closer to healing and getting a Jeep. But you have to concentrate on healing; you have to want to get better."

We calculated what her various kidney levels needed to be to give her a goal to fix on. We got her to picture herself driving the Jeep. She needed a car anyway, and when your daughter's been this close to death, you're ready to give her anything if it will give her the desire to live.

Slowly, her kidney chemistry came back into balance, and after a long recovery road, she got well. I believe that her strong mind was a real help in the healing process.

Adrienne is now two years beyond this event and looking forward to going to law school. She's also traveled abroad and loved it, and she is thinking about combining her interests and studying international law.

Adrienne still tries to do too much and to do it in her own way. When she was abroad, she immersed herself in the experience; she was very empathetic with the people she saw. She wanted to understand their lives and their culture. She'd do her homework in coffee shops and cafes rather than hang around with her American travel mates all of the time.

She still has highs and lows that are higher and lower than those of her friends. She's still impulsive and a risk-taker; she's been bungee-jumping and done some other scary things.

Keep in mind that not all gifted children will be like Adrienne. Each gifted child is unique and will have individual characteristics, behaviors, and problems. Whatever type of gifted child you have, my advice to you is to enrich the environment and support the child's development, wherever it goes. You have to be involved with these children. At times, it seems that they take every ounce of strength and resourcefulness you have, and sometimes, you just have to step aside as they find their own way. And sometimes parenting them hurts.

Just remember that gifted children are deep, emotionally challenging, totally exhausting, and *just wonderful*. Enjoy them!

Appendix

Learn More About...

... Bibliotherapy

Halsted, J. W. (1994). *Some of my best friends are books: Guiding gifted readers from pre-school to high school.* Scottsdale, AZ: Gifted Psychology Press.

... Counseling Gifted Children

Kerr, B. A. (1991). *A handbook for counseling the gifted and talented.* Alexandria, VA: American Psychological Association.

Silverman, L. K. (Ed.). (1993). *Counseling the gifted and talented.* Denver, CO: Love Publishing Company.

... *Creativity*

Books

Piirto, J. (1998). *Understanding those who create (2nd ed.).* Scottsdale, AZ: Gifted Psychology Press.

Sternberg, R. J. (Ed.). (1999). *Handbook of creativity.* New York: Cambridge University Press.

Sternberg, R. J. (1995). *Defying the crowd: Cultivating creativity in a culture of conformity.* New York: Free Press.

Internet Resources

American Creativity Association
www.becreative.org

Center for Creative Learning
www.lightly.com

Destination ImagiNation (affiliated with Odyssey of the Mind)
www.destinationimagination.org

Future Problem Solving
www.fpsp.org

Invent America
www.inventamerica.com

... *College Planning*

Berger, S. L. (1998). *College planning for gifted students (2nd ed., Rev.)*. Reston, VA: The Council for Exceptional Children.

Featherstone, B. D., & Reilly, J. M. (1990). *College comes sooner than you think: The essential college planning guide.* Scottsdale, AZ: Gifted Psychology Press.

College applications, scholarship information, and more
www.collegenet.org

... *Curriculum Contracts*

Winebrenner, S. (1992). *Teaching gifted children in the regular classroom.* Minneapolis: Free Spirit Publishing.

... *Curriculum Options*

Assouline, S., Colangelo, N., Lupkowski-Shoplik, A., & Lipscomb, J. (1999). *The Iowa Acceleration Scale.* Scottsdale, AZ: Gifted Psychology Press.

Borland, J. H. (1989). *Planning and implementing programs for the gifted.* New York: Teachers College Press.

Colangelo, N., & Davis, G. A. (1997). *Handbook of gifted education (2nd ed.).* Boston: Allyn and Bacon.

Daniel, N., & Cox, J. (1988). *Flexible pacing for able learners.* Reston, VA: The Council for Exceptional Children.

Davis, G. A., & Rimm, S. B. (1997). *Education of the gifted and talented* (3rd ed.). Boston: Allyn and Bacon.

Gallagher, J. J., & Gallagher, S. A. (1994). *Teaching the gifted child (4th ed.).* Boston: Allyn and Bacon.

Reilly, J. M. (1992). *Mentorship: The essential guide for schools and business.* Scottsdale, AZ: Gifted Psychology Press.

Smutny, J. F., Walker, S. Y., & Meckstroth, E. A. (1997). *Teaching young gifted children in the regular classroom.* Minneapolis: Free Spirit Publishing.

Van Tassel-Baska, J. L. (1998). *Excellence in educating gifted and talented learners.* Denver: Love Publishing Company.

Van Tassel-Baska, J. L. (Ed.). (1993). *Comprehensive curriculum for gifted learners.* Boston: Allyn and Bacon.

Van Tassel-Baska, J. L. (1992). *Planning effective curriculum for gifted learners.* Denver: Love Publishing Company.

... *Depression*

Partos, P. G., & Shamoo, T. K. (1989). *Depression and suicide in children and adolescents: Prevention, intervention, and postvention.* Boston: Allyn and Bacon.

... *Diversity and Multiculturalism*

Bireley, M., & Genschaft, J. (1991). *Understanding the gifted adolescent: Educational, emotional, and multicultural issues.* New York: Teachers College Press.

Cline, S., & Schwartz, D. (1999). *Diverse populations of gifted children: Meeting their needs in the regular classroom and beyond.* New York: Prentice Hall.

Ford, D. Y., & Harris, J. J. (1999). *Multicultural gifted education.* New York: Teachers College Press.

... *Enrichment*

Junior Great Books Program
1-800.222.5870
www.greatbooks.org/

Summer Institute for the Gifted
www.cpg-sig.com/

... *Gifted Children*

Books

Clark, B. (1997). *Growing up gifted: Developing the potential of children at home and at school, (5th ed.).* Upper Saddle River, NJ: Merrill.

Colangelo, N., & Davis, G. A. (1997). *Handbook of gifted education, (2nd ed.).* Boston: Allyn and Bacon.

Piirto, J. (1994). *Talented children and adults: Their development and education.* New York: Macmillan/Merrill.

Winner, E. (1997). *Gifted children: Myths and realities.* New York: Harper Collins.

Journals and Magazines

Gifted Child Quarterly (scholarly journal)
    National Association for Gifted Children
    1707 L Street N.W., Suite 550
    Washington, D.C. 20036
    www.nagc.org/

Gifted Child Today (magazine for families and teachers)
    Prufrock Press
    P.O. Box 8813
    Waco, TX 76714-8813
    www.prufrock.com/

Gifted Children Monthly (online newsletter for parents and
   teachers)
   www.gifted-children.com/

Journal for the Education of the Gifted (scholarly journal)
   Prufrock Press
   P.O. Box 8813
   Waco, TX 76714-8813
   www.prufrock.com/

Journal of Secondary Gifted Education (scholarly journal)
   Prufrock Press
   P.O. Box 8813
   Waco, TX 76714-8813
   www.prufrock.com/

Parenting for High Potential (magazine for parents)
   National Association for Gifted Children
   1707 L Street N.W., Suite 550
   Washington, D.C. 20036
   www.nagc.org/

The Roeper Review (scholarly journal)
   P. O. Box 329
   Bloomfield Hills, MI 48303
   www.roeperreview.org/

Understanding Our Gifted (parent magazine)
   Open Space Communications
   1900 Folsom Suite 108
   Boulder, CO 80302
   www.openspacecomm.com/

Internet Resources

Academic Talent/UC Berkeley—
www.atdp.berkely.edu

American Association for Gifted Children
www.jayi.com.aagc

Arizona Center for Academic Precocity
www-cap.ed.asu.edu/

Belin-Blank Center for Gifted Education and Talent Development
www.uiowa.edu/~/belinctr/

Center for Talent Development, Northwestern University
www.ctd.northwestern.edu/

The ERIC Clearinghouse
www.ericec.org/

Hoagie's Gifted Education Page
www.hoagiesgifted.org/

Lifeline to the Net's Gifted Resources Index
members.aol.com/discanner/index

Midwest Talent Search (Northwestern University)
www.ctdnet.acns.nwu.edu/

The National Association for Gifted Children
www.nacg.org/

The National Foundation for Gifted and Creative Children
www.nfgcc.org/

The National Research Center on the Gifted and Talented
www.gifted.uconn.edu/

National Research Center on Gifted and Talented (NRCG/T)
www.ucc.uconn.edu/edu/wwwgt/nrcgt.html

Rocky Mountain Talent Search
www.du.edu/education/ces/rtms.html

TAGFAM – Families of the Gifted and Talented
www.TAGFAM.org

YAHOO Resources for/about Gifted Youth K-12
www.yahoo.colm/text/education/k_12/Gifted_Youth

Your state's Department of Education

... *Gifted Children's Self-Perceptions*

American Association for Gifted Children (1984). *On being gifted.* New York: Walker & Co.

Delisle, J. R. (1986). *Gifted kids speak out: Hundreds of kids 6-13 talk about school, friends, their families, and the future.* Minneapolis: Free Spirit Publishing.

... Giftedness and Disabilities

Baum, S. M., Owen, S. V., & Dixon, J. (1991). *To be gifted and learning disabled.* Mansfield Center, CT: Creative Learning Press, Inc.

Bireley, M. (1999). *Crossover children: A sourcebook for helping children who are gifted and learning disabled.* Minneapolis: Free Spirit Publishing.

JHU Center for Talented Youth Staff (1991). *The gifted learning disabled student.* Baltimore, MD: Johns Hopkins University.

Whitmore, J. R., & Maker, C. J. (1985). *Intellectual giftedness in disabled persons.* Austin, TX: PRO-ED.

... Gifted Parent Support Groups

Webb, J. T., & DeVries, A. R. (1998). *Gifted parent groups: The SENG model.* Scottsdale, AZ: Gifted Psychology Press.

... Grants

The Foundation Center (has libraries in Atlanta, Cleveland, New York, NY, San Francisco, and Washington, D.C.) www.fdn.center.org/

The Grantsmanship Center www.tgci.com/

... *Highly Gifted*

The Gifted Development Center
www.gifteddevelopment.org/

The Hollingworth Center for Highly Gifted Children
www.hollingworth.org/

... *Homeschooling*

Dobson, L. (1999). *The homeschooling book of answers*. Rocklin, CA: Prima Publishing.

Field, C. M. (1998). *A field guide to home schooling.* Grand Rapids, MI: Fleming H. Revello Co.

Gifted Children and Home Schooling
members.aol.com/discanner/gift/home.html

National Home School Association
P. O. Box 157290
Cincinnati, OH 45215-7290

... *Legal Issues*

Karnes, F. A., & Marquardt, R. G. (1991a). *Gifted children and the Law: Mediation, due process, and court cases*. Dayton, OH: Ohio Psychology Press (now Gifted Psychology Press).

Karnes, F. A., & Marquardt, R. G. (1991b). *Gifted children and legal issues in education: Parents' stories of hope.* Dayton, OH: Ohio Psychology Press (now Gifted Psychology Press).

Karnes, F. A., & Marquardt, R. G. (2000). *Gifted children and legal issues: An update.* Scottsdale, AZ: Gifted Psychology Press.

... Multiple Intelligences

Gardner, H. (1983). *Frames of mind: The theory of multiple intelligences.* New York: Basic Books.

... Parenting

Bettelheim, B. (1988). *A good enough parent.* New York: Vintage Books.

Brazelton, T. B. (1994). *Touchpoints: Your child's emotional and behavioral development.* New York: Perseus Books.

Dreikurs, R. (1992). *Discipline without tears.* New York: Plume.

Nelsen, J., Lott, L., & Glenn, H. S. (1999). *Positive discipline A to Z (Revised and Expanded 2nd ed.).* Rocklin, CA: Prima Publishing.

... *Parenting Gifted Children*

Benson, P., Galbraith, J., & Espeland, P. (1998). *What kids need to succeed.* Minneapolis: Free Spirit Publishing.

Csikszentmihalyi, M. (1996). *Talented teenagers: The roots of success and failure.* New York: Cambridge University Press.

Delisle, D., & Delisle, J. R. (1996). *Growing good kids: 28 activities to enhance self-awareness, compassion, and leadership.* Minneapolis: Free Spirit Publishing.

Knopper, D. (1994). *Parent education: Parents and partners.* Boulder, CO: Open Space Communications.

Rimm, S. B. (1997). *Smart parenting: How to parent so children will learn.* New York: Crown Publishing.

Saunders, J., & Espeland, P. (1991). *Bringing out the best: A resource guide for parents of young gifted children.* Minneapolis: Free Spirit Publishing.

Walker, S. Y., & Perry, S. K. (1991). *The survival guide for parents of gifted children: How to understand, live with, and stick up for your gifted child.* Minneapolis: Free Spirit Publishing.

Webb, J. T., Meckstroth, E. A., & Tolan, S. S. (1982). *Guiding the gifted child: A practical source for parents and teachers.* Dayton, OH: Ohio Psychology Press (now Gifted Psychology Press).

... *Perfectionism*

Adderholdt-Elliott, M. (1999). *Perfectionism: What's bad about being too good? (2nd ed.)*. Minneapolis: Free Spirit Publishing.

... *Social and Emotional Needs of Gifted Children*

Schmitz, C., & Galbraith, J. (1985). *Managing the social and emotional needs of the gifted: A teacher's survival manual.* Minneapolis: Free Spirit Publishing.

... *Underachievement*

Rimm, S. B. (1996). *Why bright children get poor grades: And what you can do about it.* New York: Crown Publishing.

Whitmore, J. R. (1980). *Giftedness, conflict, and underachievement.* Boston: Allyn and Bacon.

Resources for Children

Barrett, S. (1985). *It's all in your head: A guide to understanding your brain and boosting your brain power*. Minneapolis: Free Spirit Publishing.

Galbraith, J. (1998). *The gifted kids survival guide (for ages 10 and under)*. Minneapolis: Free Spirit Publishing.

Galbraith, J., & Delisle, J. R. (1996). *The gifted kids survival guide: A teen handbook*. Minneapolis: Free Spirit Publishing.

Lewis, B. A. (1991). *The kid's guide to social action*. Minneapolis: Free Spirit Publishing.

Creative Kids (magazine)
    Prufrock Press
    P.O. Box 8813
    Waco, TX 76714-8813
    www.prufrock.com/

Imagine (magazine for middle and high school students)
    Center for Talented Youth
    Johns Hopkins University
    3400 N. Charles Street
    Baltimore, MD 21218
    410-516-0309
    www.jhu.edu/gifted/imagine/

References

Adderholdt-Elliott, M. (1999). *Perfectionism: What's bad about being too good? (2nd ed.).* Minneapolis: Free Spirit Publishing.

American Association for Gifted Children (1984). *On being gifted.* New York: Walker & Co.

Assouline, S., Colangelo, N., Lupkowski-Shoplik, A., & Lipscomb, J. (1998). *Iowa Acceleration Scale: A guide for whole-grade acceleration.* Scottsdale, AZ: Gifted Psychology Press.

Barrett, S. (1985). *It's all in your head: A guide to understanding your brain and boosting your brain power.* Minneapolis: Free Spirit Publishing.

Baum, S. M., Owen, S. V., & Dixon, J. (1991). *To be gifted and learning disabled.* Mansfield Center, CT: Creative Learning Press, Inc.

Benson, P., Galbraith, J., & Espeland, P. (1998). *What kids need to succeed.* Minneapolis: Free Spirit Publishing.

Berger, S. L. (1998). *College planning for gifted students (2nd ed., Revised).* Reston, VA: The Council for Exceptional Children.

Bettelheim, B. (1998). *A good enough parent.* New York: Vintage.

Bireley, M. (1999). *Crossover children: A sourcebook for helping children who are gifted and learning disabled.* Minneapolis: Free Spirit Publishing.

Bireley, M., & Genschaft, J. (1991). *Understanding the gifted adolescent: Educational, emotional, and multicultural issues.* New York: Teachers College Press.

Borland, J. (1989). *Planning and implementing programs for the gifted.* New York: Teachers College Press.

Brazelton, T. B. (1994). *Touchpoints: Your child's emotional and behavioral development.* New York: Perseus Books.

Burns, D. (1999). *Feeling good: The new mood therapy.* New York: Avon.

California Association for the Gifted (1998). *The challenge of raising your gifted child.* Mountain View, CA.

Clark, B. (1998). *Growing up gifted: Developing the potential of children at home and at school (5th ed.).* Upper Saddle River, NJ: Merrill.

Cline, S., Schwartz, D. (1999). *Diverse populations of gifted children: Meeting their needs in the regular classroom and beyond.* New York: Prentice Hall.

Cohen, L. M. (1990). *Meeting the needs of gifted and talented language minority students.* ERIC Digest (E480). Reston, VA: ERIC Clearinghouse on Handicapped and Gifted Children.

Colangelo, N., & Davis, G. A. (1997). *Handbook of gifted education (2nd ed.).* Boston: Allyn and Bacon.

Cox, J. (1985). *Educating able learners.* Austin: University of Texas Press.

Csikszentmihalyi, M. (1996). *Talented teenagers: The roots of success and failure.* New York Cambridge University Press.

Daniel, N., & Cox, J. (1988). *Flexible pacing for able learners.* Reston, VA: The Council for Exceptional Children.

Davis, G. A., & Rimm, S. B. (1997). *Education of the gifted and talented (3rd ed.).* Boston: Allyn & Bacon.

Delisle, D., & Delisle, J. R. (1996). *Growing good kids: 28 activities to enhance self-awareness, compassion, and leadership.* Minneapolis: Free Spirit Publishing.

Delisle, J. R. (1991, February 27). Aren't all children athletic? *Education Week*, Commentary.

Delisle, J. R. (1986). *Gifted kids speak out: Hundreds of kids 6-13 talk about school, friends, their families, and the future.* Minneapolis: Free Spirit Publishing.

Dobson, L. (1999). *The homeschooling book of answers.* Rocklin, CA: Prima Publishing.

Dreikurs, R. (1992). *Discipline without tears.* New York: Plume.

Dreikurs, R., & Soltz, V. (1992). *Children: The challenge.* New York: Plume.

Featherstone, B., & Reilly, J. M. (1990). *College comes sooner than you think: The essential college planning guide.* Scottsdale, AZ: Gifted Psychology Press (formerly Ohio Psychology Press).

Field, C. M. (1998). *A field guide to home schooling.* Grand Rapids, MI: Fleming H. Revello. Co.

Ford, D. Y., & Harris, J. J. (1999). *Multicultural gifted education.* New York: Teachers College Press.

Ford, D. Y., & Thomas, A. (1997). *Underachievement among gifted minority students: Problems and promises.* ERIC Digest (E554). Reston, VA: The ERIC Clearinghouse on Disabilities and Gifted Education.

Ford, D. Y. (1994). *The recruitment and retention of african american students in gifted education programs: Implications and recommendation* (RBDM 9406). Storrs, CT: The National Research Center on the Gifted and Talented, University of Connecticut.

Frasier, M. M., Hunsaker, S. L., Lee, J., Mitchell, S., Cramond, B., Garcia, J. H., Martin, D., Frank, E., & Finley, V. S. (1995). *Core attributes of giftedness: A foundation for recognizing the gifted potential of economically disadvantaged students* (RM95210). Storrs, CT: The National Research Center on Gifted and Talented, University of Connecticut.

Frasier, M. M., Garcia, J. H, & Passow, A. H. (1995). *A review of assessment issues in gifted education and their implications for identifying gifted minority students* (RM95204). Storrs, CT: The National Research Center on the Gifted and Talented, University of Connecticut.

Galbraith, J. (1998). *The gifted kid's survival guide for ages 10 and under.* Minneapolis: Free Spirit Publishing.

Galbraith, J., & Delisle, J. R. (1996). *The gifted kid's survival guide: A Teen handbook.* Minneapolis: Free Spirit Publishing.

Gallagher, J. (1985). *Teaching the gifted child.* Boston: Allyn & Bacon.

Gardner, H. (1983). *Frames of mind: The theory of multiple intelligences.* New York: Basic Books

Halsted, J. W. (1994). *Some of my best friends are books: Guiding gifted readers from pre-school to high school.* Scottsdale, AZ: Gifted Psychology Press (formerly Ohio Psychology Press).

Hoge, R. D., & Renzulli, J. S. (1991). *Self-concept and the gifted child* (RBDM9104). Storrs, CT: The National Research Center on the Gifted and Talented, University of Connecticut.

Johns Hopkins University Center for Talented Youth Staff (1991). *The gifted learning disabled student.* Baltimore: Johns Hopkins University.

Karnes, F. A., & Chauvin, J. C. (2000). *Leadership development program manual.* Scottsdale, AZ: Gifted Psychology Press.

Karnes, F. A., & Marquardt, R. G. (1999). *Gifted children and legal issues: An update.* Scottsdale, AZ: Gifted Psychology Press.

Karnes, F. A., & Marquardt, R. G. (1991). *Gifted children and legal issues in education: Parents' stories of hope.* Dayton, OH: Ohio Psychology Press (now Gifted Psychology Press).

Karnes, F. A., & Marquardt, R. G. (1991). *Gifted children and the law: Mediation, due process, and court cases.* Dayton, OH: Ohio Psychology Press (now Gifted Psychology Press).

Kerr, B. A. (1991). *A handbook for counseling the gifted and talented.* Alexandria, VA: American Psychological Association.

Kathnelson, A., & Colley, L. (1982). *Personal and professional characteristics valued in teachers of the gifted.* Paper presented at California State University, Los Angeles.

Kenny, D. A., Archambault, F. X., Jr., & Hallmark, B. W. (1995). *The effects of group composition on gifted and non-gifted elementary students in cooperative learning groups* (RM 95116). Storrs, CT: The National Research Center on the Gifted and Talented, University of Connecticut.

Knopper, D. (1994). *Parent education: Parents and partners.* Boulder, CO: Open Space Communications.

Lewis, B. A. (1991). *The kid's guide to social action.* Minneapolis: Free Spirit Publishing.

Nelsen, J., Lott, L., & Glenn, H. S. (1999). *Positive discipline A to Z (Revised and Expanded 2nd ed.).* Rocklin, CA: Prima Publishing.

Partos, P. G., & Shamoo, T. K. (1989). *Depression and suicide in children and adolescents: Prevention, intervention, and postvention.* Boston, MA: Allyn & Bacon.

Piirto, J. (1998). *Understanding those who create (2nd ed.).* Scottsdale, AZ: Gifted Psychology Press.

Piirto, J. (1994). *Talented children and adults: Their development and education.* New York: Macmillan/Merrill.

Reilly, J. (1992). *Mentorship: The essential guide for schools and business.* Scottsdale, AZ: Gifted Psychology Press (formerly Ohio Psychology Press).

Reis, S. M., Westberg, K. L., Kulikowich, J., Caillard, F., Hébert, T., Plucker, J., Purcell, J. H., Rogers, K. B., & Smist, J. (1993). *Why not let high ability students start school in January? The curriculum compacting study* (RM93106). Storrs, CT: The National Research Center on Gifted and Talented, University of Connecticut.

Rimm, S. B. (1996). *Why bright children get poor grades: And what you can do about it.* New York, Crown Publishing.

Rimm, S. B. (1997). *Smart parenting: How to parent so children will learn.* New York: Crown Publishing.

Rimm, S. B. (1994). *Keys to parenting the gifted child.* Hauppauge, NY: Barron's Educational Series, Inc.

Rogers, K. B., & Silverman, L. K. (1997, January). *A study of 241 profoundly gifted children.* Paper presented at the National Association for Gifted Children 44th Annual Convention, Little Rock, AK.

Rogers, K. B. (1991). *The relationship of grouping practices on the education of the gifted and talented learner.* (RBDM 9102). Storrs, CT: The National Research Center on the Gifted and Talented, University of Connecticut.

Robinson, N. M. (1993). *Parenting the very young gifted child* (RBDM9308). Storrs, CT: The National Research Center on the Gifted and Talented, University of Connecticut.

Saunders, J., & Espeland, P. (1991). *Bringing out the best: A resource guide for parents of young gifted children.* Minneapolis: Free Spirit Publishing.

Schmitz, C., & Galbraith, J. (1985). *Managing the social and emotional needs of the gifted: A teacher's survival manual.* Minneapolis: Free Spirit Publishing.

Silverman, L. K. (1999). *What we have learned about gifted children, 1979-1999.* Denver: Gifted Development Center.

Silverman, L. K. (1993). A developmental model for counseling the gifted. In L.K. Silverman (Ed.), *Counseling the gifted and talented* (pp. 57-59). Denver: Love Publishing Company.

Smutny, J. F., Walker, S. Y., & Meckstroth, E. A. (1997). *Teaching young gifted children in the regular classroom.* Minneapolis: Free Spirit Publishing.

Sternberg, R. J. (Ed.) (1999). *Handbook of creativity.* New York: Cambridge University Press.

Sternberg, R. J. (1995). *Defying the crowd: Cultivating creativity in a culture of conformity.* New York: Free Press.

Sternberg, R. J., & Davidson, J. (Eds.) (1986). *Conceptions of giftedness.* New York: Cambridge University Press.

Tolan, S. S. (1990). *Helping your highly gifted child.* ERIC EC Digest (E477). Reston, VA: The Council for Exceptional Children.

Torrance, E. P., & Goff, K. (1989). A quiet revolution. *Journal of Creative Behavior, 23*, 2, 136-145.

Van Tassel-Baska, J. L. (1998). Disadvantaged learners with talent. In Van Tassel-Baska (Ed.), *Excellence in educating gifted and talented learners* (p. 98). Denver: Love Publishing Company.

Van Tassel-Baska, J. L. (Ed.) (1993). *Comprehensive curriculum for gifted learners.* Boston: Allyn & Bacon, Inc.

Van Tassel-Baska, J. L. (1992). *Planning effective curriculum for gifted learners.* Denver, CO: Love Publishing Company.

Van Tassel-Baska, J. L. (1991). Identification of candidates for acceleration: Issues and concerns. In W. T. Southern & E.D. Jones (Eds). *The academic acceleration of gifted children.* New York: Teachers College Press.

Walker, S. Y., & Perry, S. K. (1991). *The survival guide for parents of gifted children: How to understand, live with, and stick up for your gifted child.* Minneapolis: Free Spirit Publishing.

Webb, J. T., & Devries, A. R. (1998). *Gifted parent groups: The SENG model.* Scottsdale, AZ: Gifted Psychology Press.

Webb, J. T., & Latimer, D. (1993). *ADHD and children who are gifted.* ERIC EC Digest (E522). Reston, VA: The Council for Exceptional Children.

Webb, J. T., Meckstroth, E. A., & Tolan, S .S. (1982). *Guiding the gifted child: A practical source for parents and teachers.* Dayton, OH: Ohio Psychology Press (now Gifted Psychology Press).

Whitmore, J. R., & Maker, C. J. (1985). *Intellectual giftedness in disabled persons.* Austin, TX: PRO-ED.

Whitmore, J. R. (1980). *Giftedness, conflict, and underachievement.* Boston: Allyn & Bacon.

Willard-Holt, C. (1999). *Dual exceptionalities.* ERIC EC Digest (E574). Reston, VA: The Council for Exceptional Children.

Winebrenner, S. (1992). *Teaching gifted children in the regular classroom.* Minneapolis: Free Spirit Publishing.

Winner, E. (1997). *Gifted children: Myths and realities.* New York: Harper Collins.

Index

D

I

J

K

L

About the Authors

Carol Strip, Ph.D., has more than thirty years' experience as a teacher, administrator, and consultant in gifted education. She is currently the Gifted Education Specialist for the Olentangy School District in Lewis Center, Ohio. In 1994, the Ohio Association for Gifted Children named Dr. Strip the Gifted Educator of the Year. She has also received the prestigious Golden Apple award from Ashland Chemical Company.

A former adjunct professor at Ashland University, Strip now serves in the same capacity at Ohio State University. She has been both teacher and consultant at the Summer Institute for the Gifted at Denison University. Her articles have been published in *The Roeper Review* and *Instructor*, and she has been a presenter at conferences of the Ohio Association for Gifted Children and the National Association for Gifted Children. She is listed in *Who's Who in America*.

Dr. Strip earned her undergraduate and master's degrees at Western Michigan University and her Ph.D. in curriculum development for the gifted at The Ohio State University, where she was a member of Phi Kappa Phi.

Gretchen Hirsch, a Phi Beta Kappa graduate of The Ohio State University, is the author of *Womanhours: A 21-Day Time Management Plan that Works.* She also is co-author, with Jay Wilkinson, of *Bud Wilkinson: An Intimate Portrait of an American Legend*, and editor of *Affirming the Darkness: An Extended Conversation About Living with Prostate Cancer.*

President of The Stevens/St. John Company, Hirsch produces award-winning business communications for clients in finance, insurance, healthcare, and education. She is also a corporate writing and speech coach. Hirsch maintains an active platform career, frequently speaking at writers' conferences on issues ranging from grammar and word usage to time management for communicators. She was founding president of The Humanities Alumni Society at The Ohio State University, and she received the Alumni Leader Award from The Ohio State University Alumni Association.